Robert L. Genua is the Director of Personnel of a Fortune-100 rated company with responsibility for worldwide personnel activities. He has more than twenty-two years of experience in personnel management.

PRENTICE-HALL, INC.
Englewood Cliffs, New Jersey 07632

A SPECTRUM BOOK

The employer's guide to interviewing:

strategy and tactics for picking a winner

by ROBERT L. GENUA

Library of Congress Cataloging in Publication Data

GENUA, ROBERT L
   The employer's guide to interviewing.

   (A Spectrum Book)
   Includes index.
   1. Employment interviewing. I. Title.
HF5549.5.I6G4   658.31'12   79–17499
ISBN 0–13–274696–4
ISBN 0–13–274688–3 pbk.

Editorial/production supervision and
   interior design by Carol Smith
Cover design by Tony Ferrara Studio, Inc.
Manufacturing buyer: Cathie Lenard

© 1979 by Prentice-Hall, Inc.
Englewood Cliffs, New Jersey 07632

A SPECTRUM BOOK

10 9 8 7 6 5 4 3 2 1

Printed in the United States of America

PRENTICE-HALL INTERNATIONAL, INC., *London*
PRENTICE-HALL OF AUSTRALIA PTY. LIMITED, *Sydney*
PRENTICE-HALL OF CANADA, LTD., *Toronto*
PRENTICE-HALL OF INDIA PRIVATE LIMITED, *New Delhi*
PRENTICE-HALL OF JAPAN, INC., *Tokyo*
PRENTICE-HALL OF SOUTHEAST ASIA PTE. LTD., *Singapore*
WHITEHALL BOOKS LIMITED, *Wellington, New Zealand*

Contents

v

Preface

Wouldn't it be nice if you could have a professional personnel manager, a person whose specialty is employment, at your side as you interview candidates for positions within your organization?

The impetus for this book comes in part from that question. For more than twenty-two years, I have been involved in recruiting employees for job openings in almost every area of specialization, from hourly workers to professionals, managers, and top executives. I have found that regardless of the complexity of the position or the level of the job, certain basic strategies and techniques can be brought to bear during the interview that can help you be more effective in making the right hiring decision. It's not easy to find and hire the right person for a particular job. It requires insight, skill, and sound judgment. Equally important, it requires a knowledge of the purpose and significance of all the tools involved in a sound selection process— application forms, interviews, reference checks, and the like.

If we analyze the interviewer's role, we find that there are two major functions that must be performed: first, you must be able to gather relevant information, and second, you must be able to interpret that information. In most employment situations, there are two or three people involved in the hiring process. In my experience, whenever I was one of those people, I was frequently called upon to provide the others with a "crash" course on interviewing.

If you are in a managerial position or are involved in the hiring process in any way, you undoubtedly spend a good amount of time with prospective employees. Whether you realize it or not, the time and effort spent on interviewing a new employee are infinitely more critical to the success of your organization than any time with the employee after he or she has been hired. If you hire the wrong person to begin with, the employee will have the odds against him or her from the very outset and no amount of training nor the best of supervision will turn the situation around.

As a result of recognizing the need that exists for a practical method of dealing with the how's and why's of the interview process, I have written this book. In the chapters that follow, I will share a number of strategies and techniques that will enable you to acquire and interpret information. I have stressed the practical face-to-face interview skills and techniques and have downplayed the psychological aspects of interviewing. Hence my aim has been to provide you with a practical method of conducting an effective interview by dispelling the mystique and by getting down to basics with the tools you will need to do the job effectively.

The concepts and methods are based on the insight that I have gained from students of management science and human behavior, as well as the practical experience that I have acquired as a professional employment manager and a manager of people.

This book will not tell you what specific approach is best for your particular situation. It will, however, provide a systematic approach that will enable you to conduct an effective interview, evaluate and interpret the data gathered from the interview, make objective final decisions on candidates, and, hopefully, better understand your own strengths and weaknesses as an interviewer.

The employer's guide to interviewing

CHAPTER ONE

The employment process

Although the primary focus of this book is on interviewing, it may be helpful first to discuss briefly the employment process to place the interview in proper perspective. Basically, a sound employment process consists of three major functions. These are recruiting, interviewing, and verifying information. Each function uses a number of tools and techniques to accomplish its specific objectives.

The prescribed sequence for carrying out the various functions of the employment process is graphically illustrated on the chart on page 4.

Recruiting

In recruiting, the objective is to attract as many qualified candidates as you can to produce the one candidate that can not only do the job but also excel at it. The search for candidates may involve the use of advertisements, employment agencies, search firms, employee referrals, or internal job posting. Whatever the sources, the object of recruiting is to identify that one individual capable of achieving outstanding results on the job.

Sometimes, regardless of how many candidates you turn up, you may not have captured the one you're looking for. All too often managers end up hiring the "best of the

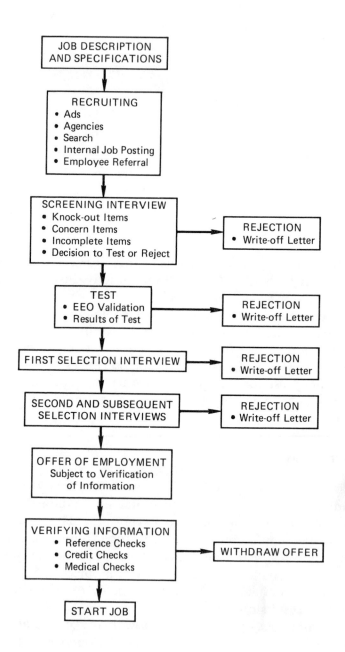

JOB DESCRIPTION
AND SPECIFICATIONS

RECRUITING
- Ads
- Agencies
- Search
- Internal Job Posting
- Employee Referral

SCREENING INTERVIEW
- Knock-out Items
- Concern Items
- Incomplete Items
- Decision to Test or Reject

REJECTION
- Write-off Letter

TEST
- EEO Validation
- Results of Test

REJECTION
- Write-off Letter

FIRST SELECTION INTERVIEW

REJECTION
- Write-off Letter

SECOND AND SUBSEQUENT
SELECTION INTERVIEWS

REJECTION
- Write-off Letter

OFFER OF EMPLOYMENT
Subject to Verification
of Information

VERIFYING INFORMATION
- Reference Checks
- Credit Checks
- Medical Checks

WITHDRAW OFFER

START JOB

4

worst" rather than going back into a recruiting mode. Don't let this happen to you. If you feel that you have not identified the one candidate that meets your requirements, then get right back into recruiting by running more ads, contacting more employment agencies, and interviewing more candidates.

Expediency has no place in the employment process. When you hire someone, it is for a long period of time, so don't rush into something you may regret.

Interviewing

Once you have identified what appears to be viable candidates, the next step is to narrow the field. This is accomplished by conducting screening interviews.

The screening interview

The objective of a screening interview is to eliminate from further consideration applicants who lack the necessary job qualifications. Because it is sometimes difficult to judge a candidate solely on the basis of a résumé or application form, it is often necessary to invite applicants for a short interview. Within the space of one half hour, you should be able to identify quickly and to rule out obviously unqualified applicants.

To prepare for the screening interview you must analyze the employment application and/or résumé. I myself very rarely interview a candidate unless I have both a completed application form and résumé on hand. The application forms I use contain blocks that require dates of employment, salary history, and past job titles. This information allows me to conduct a thorough study of the applicant before the interview, as well as to organize my thoughts and to prepare questions beforehand. During the screening interview there are three basic items to look for.

These are "knock-out" items, "concern" items, and "incomplete" items.

KNOCK-OUT ITEMS

All positions have certain minimum requirements that automatically exclude applicants. These can be called knock-out items in that they "knock-out" the applicant from further consideration. Some knock-out items that will be evident on the application form are:

- lack of experience or training

- job-related health problems

- unavailability to start employment within a reasonable period of time

- unrealistic salary expectations.

Whenever an item on the application is judged to be a knock-out factor, then the applicant should be rejected from further consideration and nothing further is required except a polite write-off letter. I strongly recommend that all rejected applicants receive a write-off letter thanking them for their interest in your company and wishing them success in their job hunt.

CONCERN ITEMS

Quite frequently, as you review the application form or a résumé, you will get an uneasy feeling that something is not as it should be. These items are referred to as concern items. Concern items warrant further exploration during the screening interview to uncover additional information about the applicant that may cause you to upgrade or to downgrade the candidate for further consideration. Some typical concern items that you might look for include the following:

- periods of unemployment—why?

- questionable reasons for leaving previous jobs—is there a pattern?

- frequent job changes—is this person a job-hopper?

- unusual salary progression—how has the applicant's salary progressed compared with others in the same career pattern?

- failure to account for all time periods—are dates conflicting or incomplete on the application?

- time lapses in education programs—was there a break in the candidate's education? Why is it incomplete? Did it take longer than usual to get a degree and why?

As you prepare for the screening interview make notes directly on the résumé or application form. These notations will serve as a reminder of the critical concern items that you should explore during the screening interview.

INCOMPLETE ITEMS

The third basic item to look for is the incomplete entry. Most application forms in use nowadays only call for limited information. You should thoroughly check the application to ensure that it is complete. All information asked for on an application form must be considered important, otherwise it wouldn't be there in the first place. If an applicant overlooks or neglects to fill out a major portion of the application blank such as salary history, education, or reasons for leaving, it is best to ask him or her to write in the missing information *before* you start the interview. If there are only one or two blanks, however, you may want to fill in this information during the course of the interview.

The same techniques that are used in conducting a selection interview are used for the screening interview. Since an overview of the selection interview is covered later in this chapter and in-depth later in the book I will not go into it here. As you conduct the screening interview, however, you will most likely be comparing candidates against predetermined criteria. That comparison will allow you to identify quickly applicants either for further consideration or rejection. When you decide to consider the applicant further, you will want to test the candidate if your company uses selection tests. In the past several years the use of tests as a selection tool has decreased somewhat due to the need for validating tests to comply with equal employment opportunity requirements. If, however, your company does test and you decide the applicant should be tested, you can introduce the subject by saying something like, "I very much appreciate the opportunity I've had to talk with you today. It appears to me that you have some of the qualifications for the job. The next step will be for you to take our employment tests. This will give me a better understanding of your qualifications and will also give me an idea of the likelihood of your chances for success with our company."

If you make the decision to reject the applicant, it is best to avoid telling him or her of your decision outright. Instead, you should thank the applicant for his or her time and advise that he or she will be hearing from you within a specified time. Although it is desirable that the applicant knows where he or she stands at the end of the interview, verbal turndowns simply do not work. A verbal turndown at the end of an interview can lead to problems such as discrimination complaints or letters of complaint to company officials.

One of the difficult aspects of the verbal turndown is that the applicant frequently wants specific information as to why he or she was rejected. Only the most skilled person is able to provide a response which is general enough to avoid specific reasons for rejection and yet provide one that satisfies the applicant. I recommend the following approach in lieu of a verbal turndown. At the end of the interview thank the candidate for his or her time and tell him or her that you "will be interviewing a number of candidates after which time you will be analyzing the results. Based on those results a decision will be made and all candidates will be advised of the results."

I have found this approach works very well since it avoids any reference to a candidate's deficiencies, provides recognition of the fact that there is competition for the job, and implies that everyone is in the running until a winner is declared. People accept coming in second or third but do not accept not being able to participate in the game by being eliminated at the start. So, it's important to let them down gracefully.

The selection interview

The selection interview is the third step in the employment process. Its function is to gather data on the applicant so an evaluation can be made. Frequently, two or more selection interviews are required to evaluate a candidate thoroughly.

One of the difficulties in interviewing is that the job applicant rarely presents his or her full "real self," but rather the image that he or she feels you are seeking. Consequently, the skill involved in interviewing is the key variable in utilizing the interview in the selection process. A well-conducted interview is a valuable tool in the employment process. A poorly conducted interview is not. Any judgment made or influenced by an unsound or ineffective interview is unfair to the applicant and ultimately unfair to your company. In the following chapters I will cover the skills and techniques that when applied will enable you to conduct a productive, effective interview.

Verifying information

Throughout the employment process you will be gathering information. You will have obtained both written information such as the applicant's résumé, application form, and letters of recommendation and verbal information from the interviews. The burden then falls on you to confirm that information. The tools used to confirm or to verify information are reference checks, credit checks, and medical examination. All of these will be discussed in further detail in the following chapters.

In the chapters that follow, I will focus on the area of the employment process that deals with selection interviewing.

CHAPTER TWO

Developing a selection strategy

What, one may ask, is the profile of an ideal candidate, the one that will most likely be offered the job? Before interviewing any candidates, you should focus on what it is you are looking for. Everyone involved in the recruiting process should have a clear understanding of the profile or characteristics of the specific person who is being sought. Here is why. Generally, the most effective managers have the most effective organizations. These organizations, in turn, are comprised of people who possess definite skills, attitudes, abilities, experiences, and personalities. In many instances, however, it is the specific individual differences that enable the manager to mold an effective team in which the strengths and weaknesses of each individual member balance with those of each other member so superior performance results. For example, one member of the team may be an outstanding planner, but when it comes to executing the plan, he or she may only be average. Another team member, strong in execution, can make the plan a reality and can obtain the desired results.

Professional managers do not recruit people to be effective performers only. They seek the specific applicant who will maximize the effectiveness of the team. Therefore, if you know the characteristics you are seeking in an applicant, you can then begin to develop a selection strategy or hiring plan. The development of such a strategy will materially assist you in hiring the right person for the right job. But, it cannot be done in a vacuum. It must be done in concert with all other members of the team involved in the final hiring decision. All interviewers must have a clear understanding of what it is they are seeking, and everyone must be on the same track in seeking the specific applicant that will ultimately be hired.

Inter-interviewer reliability

The team approach to developing a selection strategy, for use during the interview process, helps to achieve a higher degree of objectivity among the members of the team doing the interviewing. When all members in the interviewing "loop" are familiar with the criteria for the position, they can then compare each candidate within the same frame of reference. This injects a higher degree of accuracy into the judgment of the interviewing team, and their ability to predict the chance of success for any given applicant is greatly enhanced.

Developing the strategy

The three major elements that form the basis for developing a strategy are the person, the job, and the company.

The person

An effective method that I use to describe a person consists of dividing the description into three parts. The first part consists of the applicant's past history, the second of the present set of personal characteristics, and the third of future potential. The past history consists of the obvious phases of the person's life story—job history, education, experience, health, and so forth. In describing the person, you establish a broad profile that describes in general terms the basic requirements that are needed. The second part of the description deals with the person's psychological make-up—his or her personality and characteristics that differentiate that person from everyone else. And, finally, every person has a future potential that derives from his or her past history and psychological makeup. These three areas, when combined, give us a pretty clear idea of the kind of candidate we are seeking. All that remains now is to put it into concrete terms.

First, let's pin down past history by specifying pertinent past experience that the applicant will need to be successful on the job; formal education required to meet the intellectual requirements for success; degree of health needed to meet the physical demands of the job; and job history in terms of relevancy, transferable skills, salary progression, level of responsibility, advancement, and overall track record.

The first part of your selection strategy may look like this:

PART ONE—THE APPLICANT'S PAST

education:	level and type of degree(s)
training:	amount and type
work experience:	number of years functional area business or industry type and size of companies
skills:	type and level of proficiency
community activities:	involved/not involved
hobbies/interests:	active/inactive

Part two of establishing the candidate's profile involves looking into the various aspects of the personal makeup of the person. This can be done by listing words and phrases that describe the qualities you are seeking. Here are a few examples of what I mean:

mental effectiveness	decisive
aggressive	inspire others
production-minded	tact
tough-minded	social sensitivity
self-confident	above average intelligence
courage of convictions	good verbal ability
take-charge type	good numerical ability
organizer	can improvise
analytical thinker	flexible
critical thinker	infectious enthusiasm
good judgment	sense of humor
long-range planning ability	persuasive
strategic planning ability	friendly
breadth of experience	extroverted
good perspective	introverted
perceptiveness	warm
can see big picture	growth potential
mechanical aptitude	communicator
good spatial visualization	leader
creative	decision maker

methodical	high energy level
good at details	money motivated
patience	needs to achieve
practical	

This list contains but a sampling of the many descriptive phrases or words that can be used in developing the profile of a candidate. In developing your profile, you must choose those phrases that best describe your ideal candidate. In a later chapter of this book, I will show you how these descriptors are used during the interview process and in the evaluating process to arrive at a sound selection decision.

PART THREE—THE APPLICANT'S FUTURE

Knowing where the applicant has been and knowing where the applicant is at present aren't good enough. We have to carry the process one step further. We must get out our crystal ball and gaze into the future. We take a look at what it is the applicant will have to do once he or she is on the job. It isn't enough to read a job description and let it go at that. All aspects of the job must be considered. For example, depending upon what is required in the job, look at the examples listed below and ask yourself if the applicant will be able to:

travel	execute plans
work overtime	relocate to another area
lead meetings	lead others
keep up with a heavy workload	contribute to special projects
get promoted	plan work
display introspection	direct projects

gain confidence of
   superiors

coordinate activities

make group presentations

get along with peers/
   superiors/ subordinates

support affirmative action
goals

Upon formulating your selection strategy, you should now have a clear picture of what the successful candidate should be. The other team members involved in the selection process should also have a clear idea of who you are looking for. If done properly everyone will have the same understanding; and I will guarantee you that when the best candidate comes along, you will recognize him or her, and so will everyone else in the interviewing loop.

Tools of the trade

In implementing your selection strategy there are certain tools at your disposal. These are: résumés, application forms, reference checks, recommendations from past employers, background investigations, physical examinations, credit checks, employment tests, work samples, and professional affiliations.

In addition to the above, recommendations resulting from other interviewers involved in the selection process should provide you with sufficient information enabling you to determine to what degree the applicant matches your selection criteria. Although you may be familiar with most selection tools, a few words are in order about their value.

The résumé

The résumé or curriculum vitae, as it is sometimes referred to, is the most widely used vehicle for communicating an applicant's background and experience to a potential employer. An examination of the résumé will allow you to make an initial screening against the selection strategy criteria. Very often, however, you will find that vital information such as salary history is omitted from the résumé thus requiring you to seek this information by other means. The best way to accomplish this is to require the applicant to complete an employment application.

The employment application

The employment application will provide you with an initial general picture of the applicant's background and experience. It fills most of the voids generally found in a résumé. The application blank also suggests areas for investigation during subsequent interviews. It should be filled out completely since it often becomes a basic document in the employee's personnel records, as well as a basis for reference and background checks. Frequently you will find applicants who balk at filling out applications or some who will write "see résumé" on the form. In cases like that, I usually hand the form back to them for completion if they left out key information such as salary history or past working experience. If they have omitted a minor piece of information, such as hobbies or supervisor titles, I will query them during the interview for that information and will fill it in myself. This procedure is recommended as opposed to setting up a confrontation type of situation which can adversely affect the outcome of the interview.

Reference checks

All references given on an application form must be checked. Keep in mind, however, these reference checks will most likely prove favorable, since the applicant will, of course, choose only those who will provide a favorable recommendation. Reference checks should be made by the hiring manager to ensure a thorough job is done. If the checking is left to the Personnel Department, you may end up with a shallow review. After all, the Personnel Department is not responsible for the success or failure of your department. So why should they devote the time and effort required to conduct an in-depth reference check? They are more interested in getting the "check" done by completing a form than they are in uncovering any weaknesses in the applicant's prior work history. So, if you want the job done right, do it yourself. Some tips on conducting reference checks are provided in Chapter Fourteen.

Prior supervisor reference checks

Because job candidates usually only list favorable references, you should advise each candidate that prior supervisors may be contacted. Further, the candidate should be advised when that will occur. If a person is presently employed, at his or her request the employer should not be contacted until a decision is imminent. On receiving the applicant's agreement, it is recommended that you contact the prior supervisor and complete a reference check.

Background investigations

If your company uses the services of an investigation company to check out and to verify information given on employment applications, then you should be aware that public law 91–508 requires that applicants be advised that a routine inquiry may be made during the employment process concerning their character, general reputation, personal characteristics, and mode of living. At the time of the application, employees must be advised that such an inquiry may be made. The results of the inquiry are then used as additional information on which to base a decision in the selection process. In the event that the investigation is not completed prior to the employee's starting date, and the investigation reveals disqualifying information, the employment offer can be withdrawn.

Physical examinations

Most companies require a pre-employment examination of all new employees. The results of that physical examination are usually reported to the personnel manager. In the event that the candidate does not pass the examination, the offer of employment can be withdrawn.

Credit checks

If your company uses the services of a private organization to verify the financial responsibility aspects of a potential employee, then that information, if highly unfavorable, can be a consideration in the final hiring decision.

Employment tests

Many companies use various employment tests to measure the degree of skill that potential employees possess. Tests are also used as predictors of expected performance on the job. They also help to clarify information revealed in other parts of the selection process; but more important, they can provide new relevant information about the candidate not normally uncovered in an interview.

In many industrial situations testing acts as a barrier that applicants must hurdle for admission. Research indicates that much of the possible value of tests is ignored if they are used in a limited way. When the extensive information base of tests is more properly used as a guideline for other parts of the selection process, the potential of the entire process is greatly increased.

If your company uses tests in the employment process, then you should view them beyond the mere pass-fail function. To assist you in that regard, some basic information on the nature of tests and test usage is presented here.

A test is a measuring device designed to show you a small slice of the applicant's characteristics, taken under fairly standardized and uniform conditions. Through research and equal employment opportunity validation, this slice is carefully selected to predict a broad area in which the applicant will have to perform on the job. Further, the tests must be "valid" in the sense that they measure characteristics that are indeed required for success on the job.

In the realm of employment testing we used to hear the criticism, "I don't see what difference it makes if a person can solve paper-and-pencil problems or not, since he or she does not have to do that on the job." This is no longer the case since each and every test given to applicants must be job related or you can run afoul of the equal employment opportunity laws and regulations. Assuming that your tests have been validated, and further that the test items have been properly selected, it has been proven by years of research that tests are valuable aids in making predictions on a person's future performance. The value of tests lies in the ability of the tests to get at certain kinds of information. Differences in appearance are quite obvious. Differences in background, experience, and education are easy to determine from the application form and from the interview. Differences in basic abilities, interests, and values are less obvious and more difficult to estimate by these methods. It is in these areas that tests can make the greatest contribution by providing an accurate and efficient means of measuring these important characteristics.

Work samples

Work samples serve as concrete evidence of a person's ability to perform such functions as writing, graphics, advertising, sales promotion, and professional publishing.

They are generally called for when recruiting for a position that involves clearly defined skills.

Professional affiliations

The membership in and the participation of a prospective employee in pertinent professional affiliations provides the interviewer with additional insights into the candidate's interests and career enrichment.

The many tools that are available and at your disposal for use in the selection process should be brought to bear on your thinking in the final decision-making process. The offer of employment to a person carries with it a long-term commitment on the part of your company to that individual. Chances are that the person to whom you make an offer of employment will most likely, during his or her tenure with your company, pass from under your supervisory control to that of another supervisor. That being the case, you owe it to both the company and to other managers to ensure that all available tools at your disposal have been used in selecting the best person for the position.

Now that we have covered some of the basics involved in the employment process, let's focus in on the primary subject of this book, the interview itself. In the next chapter we are going to get into the nuts and bolts of interviewing by looking at the various ways of asking questions and the reasons for doing so.

CHAPTER THREE

Techniques of questioning

Questions asked during a job interview form the single most important element of the process. They are the primary vehicles used to gather information about the candidate. The amount of information that is gathered and the quality of that information depends to a great extent on the techniques that are used in the questioning process. Simply stated, it is not enough to ask good questions. Rather, the questions, in addition to being good, must be asked in a manner that elicits a response that provides relevant and meaningful information about the candidate.

As a background for understanding effective questioning techniques, let's take a look at several ineffective ways of asking questions. I have found these mistakes in questioning technique to be quite common among inexperienced interviewers. Here are some of them.

- asking too many questions that can be answered merely "yes" or "no," which can come through as an interrogation

- asking a series of routine, unimaginative questions for which a sharp applicant has already prepared answers

• asking leading questions that suggest the "proper" answer to the applicant, such as, "It appears that you left your last position for money" or "Your past experience suggests that you enjoy traveling, do you?"

It should be noted here that leading questions can be used effectively if they set the stage for a second question that causes the applicant to clearly take a position, such as, "It appears that you didn't like your last job, did you?" followed by, "What didn't you like about it?"

There are other situations to avoid. For example:

• Don't ask questions or make comments that reveal your own attitude or feelings, such as, "That was a good reason for getting upset with your employer" or "What has been your experience in dealing with those hard-nose bosses who insist on your getting to work on time in the morning?"

On the other side of the coin, there are certain comments that can reveal an unfavorable attitude on your part to a remark made by an applicant. Those comments could create a barrier to further open expression of ideas. The worst case would be wherein your comments would put the candidate on the defensive, resulting in minimizing the effectiveness of the interview.

Some examples of comments that could create an unfavorable reaction are, "If you had to do it over again, would you make the same mistakes?" or "That wasn't very wise, was it?" or "That wasn't a good reason to quit your job, was it?"

• Don't ask questions that are already answered on the résumé, application form, or in other correspondence with the applicant. Those questions do not add anything to your data collection and waste valuable time.

- Don't ask questions that are not related to the job nor the task at hand, such as, "What do you think of this weather we're having?" or "How was the traffic on the way here today?"

That type of approach, which is used to establish a relationship with a candidate, only postpones the inevitable job-related questions and may serve to intensify the applicant's uneasy feelings rather than to minimize them. The applicant may be thinking, "Let's get going with this interview, the suspense is unnerving."

The basic question— direct and open-end

There are many fine distinctions that can be made between questioning techniques, such as reflective, interpretive, summary, leading, echo, and inferential. Although I will discuss some of these in more detail later, my purpose here is to focus on two basic types of questions that can be used most effectively by you in the interview.

The direct question is simply a question that can be answered adequately in a few words. Examples include:

- How long did you work as an accounting specialist?

- What was your favorite subject in college?

- What was your salary when you left that position?

On the other hand, the open-end question usually requires more than a few words for an adequate response. This type of question is designed to give the applicant lots of room in answering. Some open-end questions are:

- Would you tell me about your career since graduating from college?

- How would you describe yourself?

- What do you feel are your strengths?

Both types of questions have their place in an effective interview. The direct question is often needed to draw out specific information. On the other hand, too heavy a reliance on direct questions can make the interview appear to the applicant like an interrogation process and may tend to cause the applicant to become defensive. Also, the applicant will often recognize what you are seeking through a series of direct questions and may be able to anticipate them, which would provide ample lead time to formulate an acceptable answer.

When probing for information about an applicant's attitudes, successes, failures, and so forth, the use of open-end questions is far better. It allows the opportunity for the applicant to freely express himself or herself, which in turn may give you additional clues. In addition, it will encourage the applicant to do most of the talking, and this is the key to a good interview. The more talking the applicant does, the more information you will receive. As a rule of thumb, the interviewer who takes up a third or more of the interviewing time talking is a poor interviewer. Perhaps even more basic to our earlier comments on the interviewer-interviewee relationship, the use of open-end questions conveys that you are really interested in understanding the applicant as a person and in a full expression of his or her viewpoints. There is an easy way to turn direct questions into open-end questions. All that is required is to begin your questions with phrases such as the following:

- Describe ____ .

- What were some of the reasons ____ ?

- How did you happen ____ ?

● What were some of the situations ＿＿＿ ?

These are just some of the many phrases that will tend to elicit more information from the applicant.

The key to using open-end questions is flexibility. Your task is to obtain the information outlined in your selection strategies. As a general rule you should use direct questions when specific information is required and an open-end question when you want the applicant to elaborate. Your job is to get him or her to talk freely and honestly. This technique will enable you to do this effectively.

Other types of questions

As I indicated earlier there are many fine lines that can be drawn between types of questions. I will mention two more that can be used effectively by you in a selection interview. These are reflection and interpretation.

Reflection

The reflection question is very simple to use and is very effective. It consists of repeating or rephrasing a portion of what the applicant has said. For example, suppose the applicant says, "And then I started having disagreements with my boss." You will want to know about these disagreements, so you "reflect" the question by saying, "You had disagreements with your boss?" Almost inevitably the applicant will begin to talk in more detail about any disagreements with his or her boss.

Needless to say, the reflection type of question should be used sparingly. If you use it too much, it tends to lend an air of absurdity to an interview. But intermixed with other questions, it can be useful.

Interpretation

The interpretation question is one in which you go beyond merely repeating what the other person says and attempt to interpret. You piece together what has been said and *add* something to it, hoping to move more deeply into the subject. An example would be: "Could it be that these disagreements with your supervisor resulted from the fact that he was promoted over you?" Obviously, to make such an interpretation the interviewer had to be able to relate things that the interviewee has implied but has not stated explicitly. Also, you must have a good interviewer-interviewee relationship for an interpretation question to be effective. If the applicant is defensive and tense, an interpretation question is not the one to be used. Interpretation questions require more skill than other questions, and should be used very sparingly.

Let's take a closer look at reflection and interpretation questions by following this example of a conversation:

CANDIDATE: I am interested in getting into sales because it pays more and the opportunity for advancement is greater.

INTERVIEWER: You are looking for advancement?

(Reflection)

CANDIDATE: Yes. I can do okay where I am. But I hear that advancement is faster in sales.

INTERVIEWER: Why do you feel that way?

(Open-end)

CANDIDATE: Well, I've talked to friends of mine, and they say that's the fastest way to advance in a company.

INTERVIEWER: Your friends have convinced you that it's the best way to get ahead?

(*Interpretation*)

CANDIDATE: Yes, that's what they have told me.

INTERVIEWER: Let's talk about your present job. How is it going?

(*Open-end*)

CANDIDATE: It's going along fine; however, I don't think I'm getting anywhere.

INTERVIEWER: Not getting anywhere?

(*Reflection*)

CANDIDATE: That's right. I do my job well. No complaints. But things could be much better in a way.

INTERVIEWER: Could you tell me why?

(*Open-end*)

CANDIDATE: Well, I really like the company, and they have been good to me. I like the people, but I don't like the atomosphere there.

INTERVIEWER: You don't *like* the atmosphere?

(*Reflection*)

CANDIDATE: No, too much rush, too much paper work, and no time to think. It makes you feel like you're on a treadmill and going no place.

INTERVIEWER: Would you say more about that?

(*Open-end*)

CANDIDATE: Yes. I thought of quitting but that didn't make sense. Then I thought of selling.

INTERVIEWER: You mean that the idea of selling was born out of necessity?

(Interpretation, softened by the word "necessity")

Additional questioning will get to the applicant to reveal that he or she was forced to go into selling to remain employed.

These examples of reflection and interpretation questions are used here for the purpose of illustration. When appropriately used during an interview, they can be very effective.

Controlling the interview

If you are to conduct an effective interview, especially in regard to gathering only job-related information, it is important that you remain in total control. Say, for example, that in response to one of your questions, the applicant talks on and on, giving you more detail than you want; you should refrain from using reinforcers such as "mmhm, I see." But suppose that withholding reinforcers is not enough to make the applicant stop talking. What would you suggest doing then? The answer to that is really simple, you interrupt him or her! The nicest thing to do is to wait for a pause at the end of a sentence. Then jump in with a neat transition such as, "Well, that tells me all I need to know about your educational background; now could we go on to discuss your work experience?"

If the applicant is a continuous talker and simply doesn't pause long enough for you to interrupt, you may have to interrupt him or her in mid-sentence. This may seem to be disastrous for rapport, but it isn't. The nonstop talker is equally responsible for rapport and will have to give and take to maintain it and to get on with the interview.

Up to this point I have discussed the use of the most commonly used questions: direct, open-end, reflective, and interpretative. I have also talked about the importance of control throughout the interview. In the next chapter I will discuss some of the techniques for using these questions.

CHAPTER FOUR

The screening interview

The selection process is basically a process of elimination. You start out by gathering as many résumés and employment applications as you can, and then one by one you whittle them down until you feel that you have captured your ideal candidate. At that point, however, you may find that you have several candidates that are equally qualified: hence you will want to interview all of them. But, because the interview process is hard work and time consuming, you probably will not want to tie up a lot of management time unless you absolutely have to. What then is the answer? Simple. You vary the length of the interview depending on your level of interest in the candidate. Your initial meeting with each candidate can be kept to thirty minutes. This will allow you to interview six to eight applicants in a day, or if you have to, you can see as many as sixteen but that would be pushing it and your effectiveness might suffer. I have on occasion conducted "marathon" interview sessions in which I have interviewed up to eighteen candidates in one day. I must admit, however, that by the end of the day I was exhausted, and quite frankly had I not taken copious notes on each candidate, I would not have remembered several of them.

During a normal day, however, the screening interview is an excellent means of seeing a large number of people in a short period of time. To ensure that the applicant understands how long the interview will last, you should tell him or her at the start. One can generally start the interview by saying, "Hi, I'm so and so. Today I'd like to chat with you for about thirty minutes . . . ." By providing that information initially, it is relatively easy to close the interview after the thirty minutes are up without creating any feeling of abruptness or lack of interest in the candidate.

The second and subsequent interviews with those candidates who survived the screening interview will be progressively longer and in greater depth as you continue to whittle down the field to that one person who best meets your requirements. A word of caution is in order here. Never under any circumstances hire the best of the worst. This means that you may not have captured your ideal candidate in the early stages of gathering applications and résumés, and hence your whittling down process was all in vain. If at the end of the elimination process you find that you still have not identified a suitable candidate, then you must start the process all over again. I repeat, do not hire the best of the worst.

Let's go back now and take a look at this process in greater depth and focus on some of the key points.

The screening interview is designed to take up no more than approximately thirty minutes per candidate to allow the interviewer to interview a large number of candidates. The subsequent selection interviews are designed to take anywhere from one to three hours; hence only one or two such interviews can be conducted during a normal working day.

Preparing for
the screening interview

To prepare properly for a screening interview, you must analyze the candidate's application or résumé. As mentioned earlier, a thorough study of the information provided before the interview will help you to organize your thoughts and will prepare you for the screening interview. Also, as mentioned earlier, you must study the applicant's application and résumé and look for knock-out, concern, and incomplete items. If there are any minimum requirements that the applicant does not meet, then the candidate is eliminated. These minimum requirements are designed to exclude automatically anyone who fails to meet them. Some knock-out items that may be evident from an applicant's papers can be lack of experience or training, job-related health problems such as overweight, unavailable to start employment within a reasonable period of time, or unrealistic salary expectations.

You must also pinpoint the concern items that will warrant an explanation. If you are concerned that something is not as it should be, then you must check it out. Further exploration of concern items during the interview may uncover additional information about the applicant that could cause you to raise or lower your evaluation. Once again, some typical concern items that you should look for include periods of unemployment; questionable reasons for leaving previous jobs (is there a pattern?), frequent job changes (is the person a job hopper?), unusual salary progression (how has this person's salary progressed in relation to that of others in the same career pattern?), failure to account for all time periods (do the dates conflict or are they incomplete on the application?), was there a break in the candidate's education? (why is it incomplete? Did it take longer than usual to get the degree? Why?)

As you prepare for the interview, make your notes directly on the application or résumé. Your notations will serve as a reminder of the concern items that should be probed during the screening interview.

You must also address the matter of incomplete items. Thoroughly check the application to ensure that it is complete. If an applicant overlooks a major part of the application blank, it is best to ask him or her to write in the missing information before you start the interview, or as mentioned earlier, if there are only one or two blank questions, you may want to fill this information in yourself during the interview.

Conducting the screening interview

The screening interview is conducted in the same manner as the selection interview which will be discussed in detail in the following chapter. The major difference between the screening interview and the selection interview is that the shorter duration of the screening interview does not permit the interviewer to explore all aspects of the applicant as deeply as he or she .could during the longer selection interview. As a result, the interviewer has to be able to identify quickly applicants to be considered further and those to be rejected.

There are a number of basic factors that can be used which will help you to identify applicants quickly and to make a judgment on them one way or another. These factors can be drawn from your original selection strategy, or they can be basic factors such as: aggressiveness, enthusiasm, responsibility, maturity, intellectual ability, personal relations, and communications skills.

Quantify your judgment.

An invaluable aid that can be used to help you to quantify your judgment is to create a matrix consisting of the factors and the applicants, and then rate each applicant against each factor. For example, suppose you have three applicants named Brown, Smith, and Jones, and you are comparing them against five factors such as aggressiveness, enthusiasm, maturity, intellectual ability, and personal relations. If you were to rate them on a scale of one to five, with five being high, your matrix would look like this:

	Candidates			
	A	B	C	D
Energy level	5	5	4	5
Ability to set high goals and be committed to them	3	5	4	4
Self-confident and positive attitude	3	5	4	5
Enjoy risk taking	4	5	4	4
Achieve success in competitive environment	3	5	4	4
Initiative	3	5	4	5
Consistently meet or exceed quotas	3	5	3	4
Express ideas precisely	2	5	3	4
Enjoy problem solving	3	5	4	4
Sensitivity to others	5	5	3	4
Cooperation	5	5	3	4
Recognize strengths and limitations of others	3	5	3	4
Listen and respond	2	5	4	3
Effectively present information	2	5	4	4
Learn quickly	2	5+	4	4
Think logically	2	4	4	4
Analyze problems	3	4	4	4
Develop new ideas	3	5	4	4
Exhibit curious behavior	3	4	4	5
Do thorough job on each task	2	5	5	4
Maintain integrity	5	4	5	5
Work independently	3	5	5	4
Maintain composure	3	5	4	4
Recognize problems	3	5	3	4
Work effectively with others	3	5	4	5
Plan and organize time	3	5	4	5
Did I personally like him/her	2	5	3	4
Is candidate a two-stepper (promotable?)	1	5	2	4
Would manager W like him/her	1	5	3	4
X like him/her	1	5	3	4
Y like him/her	1	5	3	4
Z like him/her	1	5	3	4
Performance at sales school	2	5	3	4
Top half	2	5	2	4
Is he/she better than what we have	2	5	2	3
Would I hire to work for myself	1	5	2	3
TOTAL	95	176	127	148

The matrix when completed gives you a fairly good idea of how each applicant stacks up when compared to the factors as well as with each other. It also allows you to see a little more clearly which applicants you wish to interview further and which ones you will want to reject. In the above example, because Brown and Smith scored close to each other on the high side, additional interviews may be in order, whereas you may want to reject Jones and not consider him or her any further.

The same matrix can be used during the selection process. It can be kept simple as shown in the example, or it can be made more sophisticated by increasing the factors and by assigning weights to each factor.

The table that follows shows an actual matrix that I have used numerous times and have found to be very effective in rating candidates, in this case for a sales position.

As can be seen from the foregoing, a quantification of your judgments can prove to be a useful tool. It not only helps you to sort out your thoughts on each candidate but also allows you to compare each with the other candidates. It also provides you with a "score" that should further aid you in ranking the candidates in relation to each other.

	Brown	Smith	Jones
Aggressiveness	5	4	3
Enthusiasm	5	5	5
Maturity	4	4	2
Intellectual Ability	3	5	2
Personal relations	2	4	3
TOTAL	19	22	15

In the next chapter I will discuss the selection interview. Those candidates that have successfully hurdled the initial screening interview will be brought back for a closer, more critical look.

CHAPTER FIVE

The selection interview

After you have completed your round of screening interviews and have whittled down the field to several promising candidates, you are ready to conduct longer, more penetrating and more complex interviews to gain the necessary insight into the candidates so that you can arrive at a hiring decision.

Obviously, good interviewing is difficult. You not only have to pay close attention to everything going on but you must also appear spontaneous in your conversation. To further compound the problem, the job applicant rarely wants to present the full "real self," but rather the picture that he or she feels you are seeking.

Consequently, the key variable in using the interview as a selection tool is the skill of the interviewer. A well-conducted interview is a valuable tool in the selection process; a poor one is not! Any judgments that are influenced by an unsound or ineffective interview are unfair to your company and to the applicant.

Effective interviewing

There are a number of criteria that can be applied to measure the effectiveness of an interview. As a minimum, however, at least four criteria must be met if the interview is to be used as a serious employment tool. They are coverage, consistency, relevancy, and clarity.

The criterion of coverage is necessary to ensure that all aspects of the candidate are explored and that they are explored to a satisfactory level of understanding. The criterion of consistency is extremely important and must be applied to ensure that the applicant's responses do not contradict what has been said previously or what has been obtained on the résumé, application, or from other sources. The criterion of relevance is important if you are to ensure that the focus of the interview is on the selection strategy factors that are relevant to success. And finally, the criterion of clarity must be applied if you are to ensure that the candidate's responses are not vague or open to more than one interpretation but are rather specific responses open to correct interpretation.

All too often managers think they are pretty good interviewers simply because they relate well to the applicant, generate a lot of discussion, apply good questioning techniques, and so on. If the information lacks coverage, consistency, relevancy, and clarity it may be poor information in terms of the selection criteria.

The role of the interviewer

There are two major roles that the interviewer must fulfill to be effective. Those roles are that of being a participant observer and that of continually forming and testing hypotheses.

Being a participant observer means that you must participate in the exchange with the candidate while you simultaneously act as an objective observer. You must be constantly alert to all verbal expressions as well as to nonverbal ones. As you participate in a face-to-face interview you must not only hear the words and observe the body language but you must also objectively evaluate everything. If you accept what you hear and see, you go on. If you have a concern or need clarification, then you must probe more deeply until you are satisfied. Any laxity on the part of the interviewer could shift this balance one way or the other resulting in the interviewer becoming more of a participant and less of an observer or vice versa. Neither is desirable if you are going to get results.

Hypothesis testing

Throughout the interview you question, listen, observe, and respond. This process is repeated until the information sought is obtained. The process itself is actually one of making and testing hypotheses. For example, during the exchange you may get a clue about how well the applicant gets along with his or her work associates. One clue is not enough to justify any conclusion the interviewer may make about the applicant-work associates relationship. Human behavior is too complex and any quick conclusions are naive. The clue provided by the applicant should lead to the formulation of a hypothesis. For example, the interviewer could establish a hypothesis that says the person will have difficulty in working with job associates. Then with a series of questions the interviewer can work toward trying to determine if the hypothesis is true or false. Thus, the skilled interviewer takes an initial bit of information and, rather than jump to any conclusion, establishes a hypothesis which he or she then attempts to confirm or deny on the basis of additional information.

The use of hypothesis also provides an excellent vehicle for formulating questions. All too often an inexperienced interviewer will encounter difficulty in asking questions. Some will even resort to a checklist. Using a hypothesis, by its very nature, and its subsequent testing can lead you into a whole series of relevant questions. For example, suppose you formulate a simple hypothesis, "This candidate will not get to work on time." True or false? Almost immediately you can come up with four or five relevant questions to either prove or disprove that hypothesis. Questions such as, What time do you usually get to work in the morning? Why so late? (Or so early?) Do you consider it important to get to work on time? Why? What is a typical work day like for you? How do you feel about the philosophy that it is more important to work smart than it is to put in long hours? (or vice versa). Has getting to work on time been a problem for you? Why? How have you resolved it?

The point here is that once you formulate a hypothesis you shouldn't have any problem in formulating the questions that will enable you to either prove it or disprove it. Quite the contrary, it will help you to keep the interview on track and moving.

With these concepts about the role of the interviewer in mind, let us now take a look at what constitutes a desirable interviewer-interviewee relationship.

The interviewer-interviewee relationship

There are a number of elements in the interviewer-interviewee relationship that directly affect your ability in the process of gathering information. Some of these elements are the climate that exists during the interview, your acceptance of the candidate, the amount of empathy that you exhibit, and the amount of pressure or lack of pressure that you exert as you question the candidate. Let's examine these elements in a little more detail. In regard to the climate it is very important that you create a proper atmosphere. It is more important in fact than many of the particulars about interviewing methods or techniques that you can bring to bear. The climate in which the interview takes place is the medium through which everything else filters. In effect it is the result of the kind of relationship that you establish between yourself and the interviewee. The basis for that relationship is the candidate's perception of your voice, manner, sincerity, attentiveness, and understanding. If you do not build an atmosphere that allows the candidate to trust and to accept you, then chances are you will not be able to gather effectively the information you need to properly evaluate the candidate.

Another element that is very important is that of showing acceptance of the candidate. Accepting the candidate with an honest regard for him or her as a person is critical to establishing the kind of relationship that will help break through the superficiality of the interview situation. Any questions that you ask and any remarks that you make must demonstrate your regard for the person. People have a greater tendency to go along with the interviewer when they feel accepted. On the other hand, when they do not feel accepted they are inclined to "clam up." It should be noted, however, that even though the interviewee accepts you, you do not have to take everything the person says at face value to gain acceptance. In other words, you can accept him or her on your own terms, and those terms must include your not relinquishing the option to question the person in depth whenever you feel the need to do so.

With regard to another element in the interviewer-interviewee relationship, I cannot stress enough the importance of establishing empathy between yourself and the candidate. It is an invaluable factor in creating a successful and purposeful conversation. Within the context of the interview or, for that matter, any other conversation, it is a conscious effort to see things from the applicant's point of view. By putting yourself in the other person's shoes so to speak, you can feel what that person is feeling and can adjust your behavior accordingly. Oftentimes people experience this with those who are close to them, particularly with members of their immediate families. When empathy is established there is an expression of congruence of feeling. When that feeling is demonstrated in an interview, the interviewee feels that he or she is being understood. That feeling encourages freedom of expression which in turn lowers the candidate's resistance to continued discussion. Furthermore, empathy enhances your ability to pick up on the other person's feelings and enables you to respond in appropriate terms. By giving the candidate the feeling that you perceive him or her correctly you will find that it results in an easier flow of the conversation. Empathy, when properly established during an interview, can be the lubricant that makes the entire process go smoothly. It must be remembered, however, that empathy requires a genuine regard for the interviewee's feelings. Displaying empathy cannot be done in an artificial manner. It is not an act. No interviewer can be fully empathetic to all interviewees any more than one could expect a person to like every other person equally well. But keep in mind that the person being interviewed is usually extremely alert to the interviewer's feelings and in turn the interviewer's tones and the genuineness of his or her conduct. You must convey by your behavior that you perceive that the interviewee considers himself or herself to be the single most important candidate that you will be interviewing.

A final element that you should be aware of concerns the amount of pressure that you exert on the interviewee. If you are going to develop and to maintain the proper climate throughout the interview you must not cross examine or use pressure tactics. Further, you must not demean the candidate or press him or her into a deficit position. Such actions invariably destroy the relationship and prove to be obstacles to the process. The interview is not the place to exert artificial pressures. Even though you feel the need sometimes to determine how well the applicant reacts under pressure, you do not have to go out of your way to create it artificially. Make no mistake about it. A well-conducted interview will provide ample opportunity to assess how a person reacts to the pressures that are inherent in the specific kind of conversation that ensues during an employment interview. Warmth, understanding, and acceptance are basic to the kind of relationship that will allow and permit full use of good interviewing techniques. Even though the ideal climate and the ideal relationship is difficult to achieve consistently and some people may cause you to turn off internally, you must be able to recognize the situation for what it is and to take those feelings fully into account when you make your judgment.

In conclusion, although there is no single best way to conduct an interview from start to finish, there are certain prerequisites to which one must adhere to be effective. First, you must strive to achieve results in terms of the four basic criteria of coverage, consistency, relevancy, and clarity. Second, you must understand your basic role of participation in the interview as you observe the candidate while you are simultaneously establishing and testing hypotheses. Finally, you must recognize that the relationship that you establish and maintain with the applicant throughout the interview is extremely important to gathering information efficiently.

CHAPTER SIX

Special questioning techniques

As we indicated in the preceding chapter, the key to conducting an effective interview is adherence to the four basic criteria of coverage, consistency, relevancy, and clarity. However, it is very unlikely that you will satisfy these criteria simply by establishing and maintaining the right interviewer-interviewee relationship and by using a variety of open-end, direct, reflective, and interpretive questions. Much more is needed to ensure that you reach the depth of understanding required to make sound judgments.

In the past I have found that all too often inexperienced interviewers frequently fail to explore appropriate areas to a depth sufficient to provide an adequate understanding. There is a reason for this. It is difficult to have to listen to an applicant while at the same time having to formulate the next question one wants to ask. The experienced interviewer, however, is much more adept at being an active listener and at being able to elaborate and to clarify the applicant's comments. Furthermore, past experiences have provided the interviewer with a "line of questioning" that enables him or her to keep the interview moving along. In a later chapter a number of such questions are provided for the reader.

It is also true that the inexperienced interviewer may

find it difficult to explore sensitive areas. These areas, when left unexplored, preclude the interviewer from gaining considerable insight into the applicant. By sensitive areas I am referring to those areas that may tend to expose some of the real person in the applicant.

Most applicants present three faces in the interviewing situation. The first face shows the interviewer what the applicant thinks the interviewer wants to see. The second face shows the applicant as he or she perceives himself or herself ideally, that is, as the applicant would really like to be. The third face, of course, is the real face of the applicant, and it is generally the most difficult to expose. When you are exploring sensitive areas to expose the true person, the applicant frequently feels threatened. For example, if you asked the applicant to tell you about disagreements with previous employers or to describe some of his or her weaknesses, or if you asked him or her for reasons that contributed to lack of success on previous jobs, you may, with these sensitive questions, create a threatening atmosphere. Yet, if the topic is relevant and if it will give you clues into the true makeup of the person, then you must explore them. Throughout the process you must continually strive to judge what's best to explore, when you can explore, and how far you can explore to gain greater insight. Much, of course, depends on the relationship that you establish. By displaying warmth, understanding, and acceptance you will elicit the cooperation of the applicant, and you will be able to greatly facilitate the exploration of sensitive areas. In some interview situations it may prove extremely difficult for you to establish the proper climate. However, if the sensitive area is relevant to the job that you are seeking to fill, then those sensitive areas must still be explored. There is no easy way to gain greater insight into an applicant. It is a matter of hard work, trial and error, and experience. There are, however, some techniques that can be used to gain greater insight and greater depth of understanding as you question the candidate.

Elaboration

Perhaps the most basic technique for gaining a depth of understanding is the use of follow-up questions that request elaboration. Whenever you feel that the candidate has made a statement that is not clear, is lacking in specifics, does not adequately cover the topic, or is too shallow or too simple an answer, then you should ask the candidate to elaborate more on the topic. This is very easy to do. Some types of phrases that you can use to request a candidate to elaborate are:

- Could you say more about that?

- Could you tell me more about that?

- Could you explain that in more detail?

- I would like to hear more about that.

- Could you give me an example of that?

- Perhaps you can clarify that for me.

All too often interviewers simply do not go far enough to clarify a topic. Whenever you feel that you are uncomfortable with a candidate's answer, then you should say to yourself, "ask the fourth question." What is the fourth question, you may ask. The fourth question is the touchstone question. What you really need to ask to know whether something is true or false, credible or not, real or illusory. It is the fundamental query that gets behind people's assumptions, and yet is the question that people usually don't ask because they assume they know the answer. By reminding yourself to ask the "fourth question" it should encourage you to continually bore in with one question after another until you reach the level of understanding that you need to pass judgment on the topic under discussion.

As you question the candidate you can occasionally use

reflective or interpretative questions that by their nature request elaboration. You can also use direct questions to key in on specific information. For example, the following is a series of the different types of questions that can be used to focus on elaborating an applicant's promotability.

INTERVIEWER: I notice that you were with your previous company four years. How did that fit in with your career goals?

(Open-end)

APPLICANT: Pretty much on schedule.

INTERVIEWER: Would you elaborate on those career goals?

(Open-end)

APPLICANT: Well, I hoped to be a manager in about four years.

INTERVIEWER: Where are you in terms of that goal now?

(Open-end)

APPLICANT: I think that I am very near to being promoted.

INTERVIEWER: Why do you say that?

(Open-end)

APPLICANT: My supervisor has told me that I am qualified.

INTERVIEWER: You feel you are qualified?

(Reflective)

APPLICANT: Yes, I think that I have the basic skills required to manage.

INTERVIEWER: Which of these skills do you feel is most important to a manager?

(Direct)

APPLICANT: I guess leadership,

INTERVIEWER: How would you describe your own leadership abilities?

(Direct)

APPLICANT: Well, I think all the people that work with me have a great deal of respect for me.

INTERVIEWER: Could you please explain.

(Open-end)

Clarification

One of the overall objectives of the interview is to explore apparent inconsistencies. These inconsistencies may have resulted from what you knew about the applicant before the interview, possibly from a screening interview, tests, or references, and what the applicant tells you during the course of the interview. To satisfy the criterion of consistency, these apparent inconsistencies have to be explored to obtain the depth of understanding that is necessary.

In addition to inconsistencies that occur between prior information and that obtained in the current interview, there may also be inconsistencies in information given during the interview itself. The applicant may state one thing in one part of the interview and may state something else in another part of the interview. You must be continually alert to recognize those inconsistencies, and you must explore them. One of the ways to do this is to point out the inconsistency to the applicant and to ask for its resolution, for example, "You indicate that your performance appraisals were very good at the Barnes Company, and yet your salary changed very little while you were there. Could you explain." Although your request for clarification can be threatening and can at times have a negative influence on the applicant's level of participation, this is not always the case. If handled properly, it can be regarded as an indication of your careful attention to detail and your sincere interest in the applicant. This will more often than not result in your being able to gain greater respect from the applicant as a result of your efforts at clarifying inconsistencies.

Repetition

Repetition is a technique that involves simply repeating a question or questions that were asked earlier in the interview and that were not answered fully. If, for example, you feel that some of the questions that you asked earlier in the interview were answered evasively or superficially or were inconsistent, then you simply repeat those questions to increase your level of understanding of the topics covered. Generally you will find that as the interview progresses and the applicant becomes less threatened and more trusting, the applicant is more likely to give you a more thorough response to the same question.

One way this can be done is simply by stating, "I realize that I asked you this question earlier, however, I would like to hear once more the reasons why you left your position with the Cougar Company before finding another job." Even though the applicant has already answered this question, by repeating it later in the interview you may gain additional insight, understanding, consistency, coverage, and clarity simply by repetition.

Looping back

At times during the course of the interview you may sense that the applicant is holding back some vital information. The more you question the applicant the more evasive the applicant becomes resulting in less and less information and more and more uneasiness on the part of the applicant. If such a situation develops then an effective technique to use is simply to drop the line of questioning at that time and to return to it later in the interview. When you return to a line of questioning you do not repeat the question verbatim. You approach the topic from a different direction. This is not as difficult as it would seem. For example, let's assume that an applicant may harbor a basic hostility toward people. You know that this is not acceptable in the employment situation. Furthermore, you feel that the applicant has erected a psychological barrier to mask it from you. This barrier might be a statement such as, "I get along very well with everybody." Because you sensed that the applicant was a little too emphatic or he or she received an undesirable score on a test measuring interpersonal relations or for any other reason that makes you sense that something is wrong, you have to store that information and return to it later on in the interview. As soon as you feel that the person does not indeed get along with everybody, you let the applicant think that you have accepted his or her claim. Later during the interview you return to your original premise, and you attack the topic from a different angle. You find yourself with an opportunity to ask the candidate about a previous supervisor, and the applicant answers to the effect that the person was rude and overbearing. By looping back you have gone around the psychological barrier and you have uncovered the fact that the applicant does not get along well with everyone.

Requesting specific examples

During the course of a typical interview an applicant is asked to describe himself or herself from a number of viewpoints. He or she is asked to describe his or her past achievements or accomplishments, strengths and weaknesses, short- and long-term goals, and monetary aspirations. Quite often you can obtain greater insight into the applicant's statements by asking for specific examples. Instead of accepting the applicant's general statements you can conduct a much more productive interview by dealing in specifics.

For example, if an applicant indicates a preference for an assignment with more responsibility and challenge and has had many such assignments in the past, you might ask the candidate to describe in specific terms the most responsible and challenging assignment that he or she has had during the last six months. By dealing in specifics you can gain a much clearer picture of the candidate. Another example would be one wherein the applicant describes himself or herself as an "effective problem solver." Once again, you can gain additional insight by asking a specific question such as, "Could you tell me what the most difficult problem was that you encountered over the past three months and what you did to solve it?"

Exploring attitudes, values, and feelings

An interviewer can gain considerable insight into an applicant by exploring the applicant's background and experience. However, a good interviewer must take into consideration the applicant's attitudes, values, and feelings. Questions dealing with background and experience can be answered by a candidate in an objective manner. On the other hand, however, questions dealing with attitudes, values, and feelings that ask for information that is not quite as factual call for a great deal of subjectivity on the part of the candidate. That subjectivity allows you to assess the candidate's attitude about such things as work, society, and politics, as well as his or her values, opinions and feelings. For example, an interviewer can focus on these more subjective items by asking questions such as "How often do you feel strongly enough about an idea that you really push for its acceptance?" "How do you feel at the end of a hard day's work?" "What motivates you to be successful?"

A frequent observation that I have made of inexperienced interviewers is that all too often they are unaware whether their questions ask for subjective or objective information. As a result, their interviews characteristically contain sequences of subjective questions, and just as the applicant starts to speak with increasingly greater depth about his or her personal convictions and really gets into the subject, the interviewer unwittingly breaks the sequence of subjective questions and starts to ask objective questions. The result? The interviewer loses a golden opportunity to gain greater insight about the applicant in terms of his or her attitudes, values, and feelings. A more experienced interviewer would have continued the sequence of subjective questions and would have gained a great deal of insight into what makes the applicant tick.

Silence

For some reason or other some interviewers find periods of silence annoying. Whenever a lull in the interview occurs they react too quickly to fill the void. However, silence for brief periods plays an important role in a purposeful conversation. The candidate may need a bit of silence to put his or her thoughts in order or to recall in sequence the information you are seeking before answering. In some cases the applicant may be blocked from responding because of an emotional situation that one of your questions may have created. Whatever the reason, by allowing a reasonable amount of occasional silence during an interview you can help to achieve the desired permissive atmosphere.

Providing this period of silence, long enough to give the candidate a chance to relax and short enough to ensure the candidate does not become uncomfortable, can prove beneficial to the conversation. In the case of the hyperactive interviewer who finds periods of silence annoying, he or she will be surprised to learn that the candidate will begin talking again quite soon after a few moments of silence. Furthermore, the use of silence may often bring out information that may not normally be asked for by the interviewer. Silence when used properly can be one of the most effective techniques of probing. It is in some respects more open than an open-end question in that it allows the interviewee to take the conversation wherever he or she chooses.

Flexibility in questioning

Since the interview is basically a conversation, the use of questions and their sequencing is a key skill of the effective interviewer. For this reason the techniques used in questioning are critical to your success as an interviewer.

There is not one fixed model for sequencing questions, since there are too many variables in the interviewing process. Such things as personality and social skills of the applicant, the type of interviewer-interviewee relationship, the type of information to be obtained, and so forth all predicate against the creation of a single fixed-skill model.

Yet, rather than avoid the subject entirely, and while recognizing the need to review what has been covered in discussing questioning techniques, a more appropriate step would be to try to summarize the general behavior of the experienced versus the inexperienced interviewer.

Inexperienced interviewers are generally fearful of being unable to keep the interview going. Sometimes, the interviewer will prepare and memorize a set of questions, even though this defeats the purpose of the nondirective interview. Alternatively, the interviewer may become preoccupied with formulating the next question immediately after asking a question. In either case, the interviewer is *listening only superficially*, at best, to what the respondent says. The interviewer is likely to show a strong preference for direct questions, even to the point of rephrasing open-end questions into direct questions.

In addition, many beginners are very fearful of silence and avoid it by jumping in with a question. The beginner also frequently interrupts a response in haste to ask the next question.

Because the interviewer is not listening carefully to what the respondent is saying and tends to focus more on the interpersonal relationship than on the response material, much of what the respondent brings up is not carefully explored through follow-up questions. Often, because the interviewer has not developed a conceptual framework in advance to guide him in selecting content, there will be many abrupt and illogical transitions. Of the variety of question techniques the interviewer will use a very limited range, with little variation within this range. The behavior of experienced interviewers, however, is quite different.

The overall impression gained by observing the experienced interviewer is that the flow of communication is smooth and that the response material is being given full and careful consideration. Rather than impose his questioning on the respondent, the interviewer adapts his pace, idiom, and thought patterns to those of the respondent. In part, the interviewer achieves this effect through relating his questions to information the respondent has given in answer to the preceding question or earlier in the interview. Because of this technique, the respondent appears to have considerable control over the topics, even when the interviewer is in fact maintaining control. The skilled interviewer follows up partial statements and cues more carefully and tolerates fewer ambiguities and internal contradictions in the candidate's responses.

In the initial stage of the interview and when introducing a new topic, the experienced interviewer often uses a number of open-end questions to get some idea of the kind of information the candidate is best equipped to provide and the manner that the interviewee finds most comfortable when providing it. The skilled interviewer is more likely to drop a line of inquiry that seems ineffective and return to it at a later time when it seems it would be more profitable.

An effective approach to questioning

An approach that I recommend is that you should use some open-end questions of broad scope early in the interview, provided that you can successfully formulate them and can specify through them the information you are seeking. If the applicant continues to produce relevant, specific information, you only need to use encouragements, and possibly clarifications, where the applicant is not clear or is too concise.

As the applicant continues speaking, you should make mental or written notes of points that need expansion or clarification, allusions that are briefly made to areas that deserve to be followed up, apparent contradictions between two responses, subtopics that have been overlooked, and so on. These can be followed up with a high proportion of direct questions and some open-end questions. In the course of such an interview, the initiative for topic selection may move between you and the applicant and may be reflected by such changes in question form as have been noted.

This approach to questioning is more nondirective. It

assumes that the average intelligent and articulate applicant prefers to share in the responsibility for topic selection and development and to express personal feelings in the manner he or she considers appropriate to the topic. Other applicants who have difficulty in organizing their ideas and expressing themselves may feel more comfortable when the interviewer more clearly structures the interview or uses a more directive approach.

The techniques of effective interviewing as discussed in this chapter are helpful in improving the reliability of the interview as a selection tool, but only if the results satisfy the basic criteria: coverage, consistency, relevance, and clarity.

In the next chapter we will see how all the strategies and techniques that have been discussed so far hang together as they are brought to bear during a typical interview situation.

CHAPTER SEVEN

A positive interview model

In this chapter I have constructed a typical interview to provide you with an opportunity to understand the thought process involved in conducting an effective interview. To do that it was necessary to use three different parts in the dialogue. The first consists of what the interviewer actually says during the course of the interview; the second includes the interviewer's thought process and provides the reader with the background for the interviewer's dialogue; the third is the interviewee's response. As you read the dialogue, and "listen in" on the interviewer's thoughts, you will gain a better understanding as to what is going on in the interviewer's mind as he digs into the candidate's background, experience, and personal characteristics. In the dialogue you will find Dick Martin, a personnel manager, interviewing a candidate, Bob Crane, for a sales position. As you read it, put yourself in the interviewer's shoes. This will help you to gain further insight and understanding as to the strategies and techniques that the interviewer is applying.

The interview

Dick Martin is Personnel Manager for the International Apex Company. As a result of earlier interviews, he has screened out all but four candidates for a sales job.

Bob Crane is one of four candidates still in the running. Whether or not he gets the job will depend to a great extent on how well this interview goes. Dick Martin's thoughts are in italics.

(D.M.): From the screening process, I've identified four candidates I think can do this job. Today, I will spend about a half hour with each one. Hopefully, I'll be able to determine whether or not I have any interest in any of them for future employment. Let's see. The first candidate is Robert M. Crane. I've read his résumé and application. He's presently waiting in the lobby. I'll ask him to come in.

DICK MARTIN: Hello, Mr. Crane. I'm Dick Martin.

MR. CRANE: Hello, Dick. Pleased to meet you.

(D.M.): First, I'll establish rapport.

DICK MARTIN: Did you have any trouble with the directions we gave you?

MR. CRANE: Oh, no. Your instructions were very clear. No problems whatsoever.

MR. MARTIN: Bob, let's go to my office, where we can chat. I'll lead the way.

MR. CRANE: Fine.

(D.M.): I prefer interviewing candidates using two chairs not quite facing each other. Interviewing over a desk creates a communication barrier.

MR. MARTIN: Have a seat, Bob. Would you like a cup of coffee?

MR. CRANE: Yes, thanks.

MR. MARTIN: How do you take it?

MR. CRANE: Oh, regular. One sugar and some milk.

(D.M.): He can sit here and relax while I ask my secretary to bring us coffee.

Dick's secretary pours them each a cup of coffee and brings it in. Dick thanks her and the interview continues.

MR. MARTIN: Bob, as you probably know we're looking for a salesperson.

(D.M.): Now tell him that you'll be taking notes, so that he won't be alarmed or concerned as you write.

MR. MARTIN: As we talk this morning, I'll be making notes on both your résumé and your application.

MR. CRANE: Fine.

The interviewer picks a point in time in the applicant's résumé or application to begin questioning the applicant.

(D.M.): Hmm. In looking over his papers, I notice Bob has been out of school for a long time. So, I don't feel it's necessary to start back in college. However, I may want to come back to that later. I think with this applicant the best place to begin would be with his first job after college. I'll ask an open-end question about that job and preface my question with a few remarks so we can lead into the interview in a comfortable fashion.

The interviewer formulates a hypothesis about the candidate. He will check out this hypothesis throughout the interview by asking questions that will either prove or disprove his hypothesis.

(D.M.): I see Bob was a manager. I'll form a hypothesis that says he is really seeking a management position and is only applying for this job with the thought of using it as a stepping stone from direct sales into management.

MR. MARTIN: As a starting point, I'd like to go back

to your first job after college. Can you tell me a little bit about that job?

MR. CRANE: Certainly. After graduating from Ohio State where I majored in economics, I was looking for a position that would make use of my educational background. At that time, the Foster and Noble Company was conducting interviews on campus, and I'd interviewed with the campus recruiter. I think during that period of time, I must have interviewed with maybe four or five various companies; however, the Foster position seemed to be in line with my objectives.

I'd been interested in marketing and Foster and Noble offered an opportunity for me to start in sales and hopefully learn the marketing field from the ground up.

(D.M.): I need more information about the Foster and Noble job so I can judge if that experience is relevant to the criteria of our opening. Specifically, I need to know if the work required a high energy level, working with high level contacts, and what his duties, responsibilities, and overall achievements were. To get at this, I'll ask him an open-end question.

MR. MARTIN: Would you tell me about your position at Foster and Noble . . . what it involved on a day-to-day basis?

MR. CRANE: I'd be glad to. I started with Foster and Noble in July, shortly after I graduated from college. I was placed in a training program, where I learned how to be a retail salesman for the packaged soap group. This position was in the north-east district. I won several district and many unit awards for sales perform-ance. As a result of that I was promoted and moved up to the position of district head salesman, oh, about October of the following year. Then I was pro-moted to district head salesman for the New Jersey area and I had to relocate. I worked on special assignments in New Jersey under guidance of the dis-trict manager, and I was completely responsible for one major chain. In addition, I successfully sold the fourth size of one product that was never carried before in that chain.

(D.M.): The fourth size of a product. What does that mean? I'm not sure I understand. I'll ask him a direct question.

MR. MARTIN: Bob, What's the fourth size of a product?

MR. CRANE: Well, we had a giant economy size, a large size, a regular size, and a fourth size called the family-size package. It fell between the giant economy size and the regular. These sizes, of course, were created by our marketing staff to meet consumer needs.

MR. MARTIN: I see. Go on.

MR. CRANE: In May I was promoted to unit man-ager, and I had responsibility for Unit C out of Colombus, Ohio. It had a sales volume of over six million dollars. At that point, I had six salespeople re-porting to me. The unit territory cov-

ered a small portion of Ohio, two coun-
ties in Kentucky and about half the
state of West Virginia.

MR. MARTIN: What else did you achieve as unit
manager?

MR. CRANE: Well, at that time, the unit had two
vacancies and was seventeenth out of
twenty-two units in the central division.
By December of that year, we had
moved up to fifth place. All sections
were filled by me, and a new brand was
introduced into the area. At that time,
all our major accounts were buying
three sizes of the products.

*(D.M.): It sounds like he was successful with Foster and Noble.
I wonder why he left. I'll ask a direct question and find out.*

MR. MARTIN: I see that you left the firm shortly
thereafter, in March. Why was that?

MR. CRANE: Basically, I left because of money. I was
earning only fifteen thousand. At that
time, an opportunity came up for me
to start my own firm, and so I did.

*(D.M.): It appears Bob left for a good reason. I'll go into his
second job, as president of his own firm. I'll ask an open-end
question.*

MR. MARTIN: I see from your application that you
were president of a firm called The
American Distributors, Incorporated in
Greenville. Could you tell me about
that firm?

MR. CRANE: Yes, as I was saying, I left Foster and
Noble to start my own firm. It was
organized by me with approximately

ten thousand dollars capitalization. I
wanted to merchandise women's ho-
siery products in drug and grocery
outlets. I handled all phases of the
operation. We were fairly successful, so
I added two people for servicing and
inventory.

*(D.M.): This guy seems to be entrepreneurial in spirit. I
wonder how well the firm did over the years and whether or
not he was successful. I'll ask him a direct question in that
regard.*

MR. MARTIN: Would you tell me about your business?
                Was it profitable?

MR. CRANE: Well, yes and no. Sales volume was
                $69,000 and then it grew over a three-
                year period to $150,000 and then it
                slid back to, well, about $36,000. I
                actually lost money.

*(D.M.): I wonder why it slid back. I'll ask an open-end
question and let him elaborate.*

MR. MARTIN: Why was that?

MR. CRANE: Well, it was a combination of three
                things. First, we were undercapitalized.
                Second, hosiery prices became de-
                pressed at all levels by 50 to 100 per-
                cent, and third, the general economic
                conditions at those times capsized the
                venture.

*(D.M.): I like the way he answered that question. Specifically,
I like the way he spelled out three reasons . . . one, two, three.
It shows he has good mental effectiveness. I don't however, like
the fact that the business failed. I need to know more.*

MR. MARTIN: What happened then?

MR. CRANE: Well, in July I sold all the accounts to a larger distributor. I might add that I got out of the business at just about the right time. The conditions I mentioned earlier got even worse before they got better.

(D.M.): The next job he had was with Corder Corporation. I'm going to lead into that now and find out what that job involved. I'll do that with an open-end question, with a little introduction for some transfer.

MR. MARTIN: I see that in August of that year, after disposing of your business, you joined the Corder Corporation. Can you tell me about that position?

MR. CRANE: Sure. I don't know if you saw the ads Corder was running at the time, but they were touting the business as being a future growth star. They were offering equity positions. I felt my background and experience plus the things I liked doing gave me a good shot at Corder. I contacted them and interviewed with them. They hired me as a regional representative.

(D.M.): Regional representative sounds to me like a direct sales job. I'll ask an open-end question and find out exactly what this job involved.

MR. MARTIN: What did your job as a regional representative involve?

MR. CRANE: I was directly responsible for handling franchise dealers. This involved answering inquiries and making sales calls on people with audiovisual authority in libraries, schools, and businesses.

(D.M.): In other words, he was actually making direct sales calls on potential customers. I need to know more. I'll ask him to elaborate and clarify.

MR. MARTIN: Tell me more about your interaction with franchise dealers.

MR. CRANE: Century had set up a number of franchise dealers in the New England states. They were independent businessmen who marketed audiovisual products directly to libraries, schools, and businesses within specific geographic territories. My job involved working with these franchise dealers and assisting them in making sales calls, so they could get their businesses up and running. Corder Corporation, the parent company, received a percentage of the revenue from each franchise dealer, so it was in their best interest for the franchise dealers to do well.

(D.M.): Well, I could have him elaborate and clarify even further, but I think I have a pretty good idea as to what his job consisted of. It was primarily interfacing with the franchise dealers and helping them close business. I have a good idea of what he was doing, so I'll ask him an open-end question as to why he left Corder.

MR. MARTIN: Can you tell me why you left Corder?

MR. CRANE: Yes, very simply. The firm ran into severe financial difficulty. And, as a result, the majority of the staff was placed on a reduction-in-force.

(D.M.): Generally, when companies place people on reduction-in-force, if there are no seniority considerations, they furlough the least productive members of the team. Could it be that Bob

*falls into that category? I'll ask him to elaborate and clarify
the situation for me.*

MR. MARTIN: About how many people did Corder
               Corporation let go at that time?

MR. CRANE: Oh, I would say in the neighborhood
               of fifteen people.

MR. MARTIN: Out of how many?

MR. CRANE: Oh, roughly out of twenty people on
               staff.

MR. MARTIN: Can you tell me why you weren't one
               of the five people they retained?

MR. CRANE: I'm not quite sure what criteria they
               used. However, I will say had they
               offered me the opportunity to stay with
               the firm, I probably wouldn't have
               done so.

*(D.M.): Well, let's see here now. This sounds a little unusual.
There must be more to the situation than meets the eye. Maybe
I'd better ask an open-end question and see what goes from
there.*

MR. MARTIN: Can you explain in a little more detail
               what you mean?

MR. CRANE: Yes, basically the situation at Corder
               was that the franchisees were running
               into a great deal of difficulty in mar-
               keting the AV product because . . .
               technically, the materials were not com-
               patible with equipment generally
               found in most AV departments in li-
               braries, schools, and businesses. As a
               result, sales were not where they
               should have been. Correspondingly,

revenues were way down. A lot of people that had invested in the business were fearful that they would lose their entire investments. At the time that Corder announced they were cutting back on staff, the severance arrangements were such that I felt it was a good time to more or less pick up my marbles and leave the game. Had they offered me the opportunity to stay on, I seriously doubt I would have. The business looked to me like it was going to get progressively worse. At the time I left Corder, I was given fairly decent outplacement assistance and, I might add, enough salary continuance to tide me over until I could find another job.

To answer your question more specifically, all I can say is that I really don't know . . . they probably had their own reasons. I don't feel the five people they retained were any better qualified or more productive than the fifteen that were let go. I can certainly assure you that my record with Corder was as good, if not better, than the people they kept.

(D.M.): Well, that was a pretty good response. I'll let him reflect on that a little and see where he goes with it.

MR. MARTIN: Then you feel you did a pretty good job at Corder and should have been retained.

MR. CRANE: Yes, I do. During the short time I was with them, I did a thorough job in covering my assigned responsibilities and any problems that developed were not my doing. Rather, the base cause of them was the failure of the products to be compatible with existing audio-visual equipment that was out in the marketplace.

(D.M.): So much for his work history. I think what I'd like to do now is get into his personality. I'll ask an open-end question.

MR. MARTIN: Would you tell me what you believe to be your strong points as a person?

MR. CRANE: Well, let me think about that for a minute. Basically my strongest point is my ability to get along with people; my peers, my superiors, and my subordinates. I've always excelled in interpersonal relations.

MR. MARTIN: I'd be interested in knowing what you believe to be some of your weak points.

MR. CRANE: Everyone has some weaknesses and I've got mine. If I were to single one out I'd probably say that it was my inability to relax away from the job. I always seem to be concerned about what's going on in my territory or what's happening back at the office. And . . . I frequently take a lot of work home with me. I have a hard time unwinding from the job and relaxing.

(D.M.): A pretty good response. In fact he used that question to his advantage. He answered it by responding in a manner that shows me his weakness is really a strength, when it comes to working. That was good.

(D.M.): Now, I think I'll ask him about qualities he admires

in other people. This will give me insight into his personality and also how he views himself.

MR. MARTIN: Would you tell me some of the qualities you admire in other people?

MR. CRANE: Yes, I think I can answer that question. Qualities I admire in other people are honesty and integrity, and above all, people who are genuine with others.

(D.M.): Well, I could use some elaborating and clarifying on that last portion. So, I'll have him elaborate by asking an open-end question.

MR. MARTIN: Perhaps you can clarify what you mean by "people who are genuine with others."

MR. CRANE: All people have strengths and weaknesses, right. But some pretend to be "supermen" or "superwomen." Often, in my business career, I've encountered people who put up a facade and try to play a role; however, it's been my experience that these people always get caught-up with in the end and are losers. On the other hand, I've worked for and with people who were genuine human beings. This came through in their everyday interactions with others. They didn't pretend to be anything other than what they were, nor did they promise anything they couldn't deliver.

The interviewer wants to hear more about this. Suspecting he may have found a negative aspect of the candidate, he probes deeper.

(D.M.): Let's get into this a little deeper. Ask some more questions, and we'll get some better insight into his character and personality.

MR. MARTIN: Can you tell me what irritates you or displeases you most in other people?

MR. CRANE: Well, I think we were just talking about that to some degree. One thing that displeases me is a person who pretends to be something he's not. Some individuals slap you on the back, then stab you in the back. I prefer an individual who is open and honest, to one who's closed and deceitful.

(D.M.): This could be a clue to his personality. I wonder if he ever really gets angry at people. I'll ask him what makes him angry.

MR. MARTIN: I'd be interested in knowing about the last incident that made you angry.

MR. CRANE: Gee, that's a tough question. I really don't recall when I've been angry the last time.

(D.M.): Well, he surely has been angry at some time in his life. Maybe I'll bounce it off him again by using a reflective question.

MR. MARTIN: You mean you haven't been angry in a long time?

MR. CRANE: Well, yes, I guess you could say that. But looking back, I think that probably the last time I got angry is when this woman left her empty shopping car in the parking lot of the supermarket. The wind caught it and it rolled into the side of my car. Not only did her cart scratch my car, but it put a dent in it.

(D.M.): I'd have to agree with him. That would irritate me, too. But I still have to find out more about his personality; so, I'll ask him another open-end question.

MR. MARTIN: Would you explain what you did about it?

MR. CRANE: Well, there wasn't much that I could do. After all, the woman didn't push the cart into my car intentionally. It was more or less an act of God—the wind caught it and it just sailed along until it banged into the car. About all I could do was get out of the car and give the woman a dirty look. Then I set the cart up so it wouldn't move anymore.

(D.M.): Well, that was a good answer. It indicates he's mature. It also shows me he has a broad perspective on the ups and downs of daily living and a tendency to look at reality squarely.

The interviewer has been satisfied up to this point. Now he seeks more relevant information and considers new hypotheses to check out.

(D.M.): I could go on and pursue character and personality to find out more about his values. I could go into the subject of money, challenge, opportunity, security. . . . I can find out if Bob is a person of convictions and quiet beliefs or whether or not he's highly prejudiced and emotional about what he thinks. I can also get some indication of his personality by just listening to the noises he makes. He sounds like a person who enjoys life and is enthusiastic, interested, and alive. There's

also warmth and a positive feeling to the comments he's making. I think I have a pretty good idea of where this candidate stands in terms of personality. The next area that I'd like to explore is ambition. While I explore ambitions, I'd like to loop back to my earlier question about whether or not this person wanted to stay in sales or whether he wanted a management role. I'll also check out the hypothesis that I formed earlier about his wanting to be a manager rather than a salesperson. I'll get at all three of these with an open-end question.

MR. MARTIN: I'd be interested in knowing what position you want to hold several years from now.

MR. CRANE: Well, as you know, for now I'm interested in a direct selling position because I feel this is where my real strengths lie. I also feel that in direct sales a person can earn more money than in management. For the next several years, I see myself as a salesperson working on some sort of incentive program where I can earn substantial money.

(D.M.): Well, he's telling me he wants to stay in direct sales for a number of years, but he still hasn't answered my question to my satisfaction. So, I'll ask him to elaborate and clarify. I'll use a direct question for this.

MR. MARTIN: In a few years from now, then, do you still see yourself in direct sales?

MR. CRANE: Yes. I see myself three years from now in an established territory with established accounts . . .selling. I don't see myself as a manager at the present time. Maybe after five years or so, I'd be ready to step into a manager's position, but not until I've proven to my own satisfaction that I'm an outstanding salesperson whose earnings are only limited by his own abilities.

(D.M): I'm still not sure I understand where he wants to be several years from now. Maybe I'd better ask him another open-end question, and check out my hypothesis even further.

MR. MARTIN: I'm not certain I understand where you plan to be in several years from now. Could you explain in a little more detail?

MR. CRANE: Yes, in a few years from now I plan to be in a direct selling position. I want my earnings to reflect my ability. And, I believe the only way this can be achieved in the short term—three to five years—is by having my salary and commissions tied directly to my performance. The only way I'm aware that this can be done, in your organization, is in a direct selling posiiton.

(D.M.): OK, that was a pretty conclusive answer. I'll ask him a question that will give me some insight into his own self-image from a subjective angle.

MR. MARTIN: Can you tell me about the reputation you like to enjoy as an employee?

MR. CRANE: I guess I can answer that. The reputation I like to enjoy as an employee is that of an honest person, a genuine human being, and a person who deals fair and square with other people. I consider myself to be a solid member of the community, and I feel I perform a useful role in society. I also consider myself to be a self-starter and a hard worker. I believe in the work ethic, and I enjoy being perceived as a contributor to bottom-line results.

(D.M.): A good answer. At this point, I can carry on the interview along the same lines, asking reflective questions and interpretive questions, open-end questions and direct questions, and getting into more elaborating and clarifying questions. I could also form more hypotheses, and I can loop to comments made earlier in the interview. I would just like to take a few moments to review this interview thus far. First of all, I'd like to reflect on this employee's appearance. How does this candidate impress me? Does this candidate create a better-than-average appearance? An excellent appearance? Does this candidate inspire me, or does he leave me cold? Is the candidate interesting or dull? Does he have personal warmth and charm, or does he repel me? Does this candidate appear neat and robust, with good posture, good facial expression? Is he tactful, courteous, confident, warm, enthusiastic, cheerful, optimistic, animated and humorous? Does the applicant have good pronunciation, enunciation, vocabulary, grammar? Does the applicant express himself freely, with clarity in an organized manner? And has the applicant exhibited good mental effectiveness, good character and personality, and good skill in human relations? Does this applicant have insight? In short, looking over this candidate up to this point, from the beginning of the interview until now, have I sensed that he is exceptional and likely to be hired? Well, I think I have, so at this point in time I will continue to interview him and get back into his individual work pattern and some of the more specific requirements of this particular position. Before I do that I'll give him an opportunity to open up new areas by allowing him to ask me questions.

Mr. Crane, you have been doing most of the talking up to this point. Do you have any questions you'd like to ask me?

(D.M.): Will he ask sharp, well-thought-out questions about the position, the company, the competition, our profitability, our growth potential or will he ask run-of-the-mill, simplistic questions? After he asks me several questions and I answer them for him, I may have a few more of my own. The more we talk, the more information I can gather.

MR. CRANE: Dick, I would like to ask you about . . . .

At this point, we will take leave of the interview model. Dick Martin will continue to use his strategies and techniques as he diligently and systematically gathers facts and relevant data that will help him to unravel Bob Crane and thus allow him to make a judgment as to whether or not Bob Crane is a suitable candidate for the opening.

One of the weaknesses you may have noticed in the foregoing interview was that Dick Martin, the interviewer, did not at times pursue the subject matter to any great depth. In fact, on a few occasions he only obtained superficial information.

In the next chapter, we will get into in-depth questioning, and we will then learn more about exploring the subject matter thoroughly and completely.

CHAPTER EIGHT

In-depth
questioning

As you probably are aware of by now a skilled interviewer must be able to pursue subject matter in depth and must be able to do so in a manner that is effective. This is a logical extension of elaborating and clarifying. By using how, why, what, when, and where, all aspects of any subject can be explored. All too often during the course of an interview, the interviewer will stop short and discontinue his or her line of questioning on a specific subject for fear that he or she will be creating a stressful situation.

There is a school of thought that says that anxiety and stress are part of many demanding jobs and by creating stress in an interview situation you may uncover clues as to how the applicant might react on the job when faced with a stressful situation. As mentioned earlier you can pursue subject matter in depth by asking the "fourth" question. The fourth question is merely an expression meaning continue to probe the subject matter at hand until you are reasonably satisfied that you have gained a thorough understanding of the information that is being sought. For example, during an interview I may ask a candidate what his or her career goals are. On hearing the response, I may need further elaboration or clarification. In other words, I would like to hear a great deal more about those career goals. My second question would be, "What are you now doing to achieve those goals?" My third question would be, "Why have you set those goals for yourself?" My fourth question would be, "What happens if you do not achieve those goals?" I may even add a fifth question and ask "What is your timetable for achieving those goals that you have set?" There are some inherent risks in conducting in-depth questioning. One of the risks is that you may create a power imbalance that may hinder the flow of information from the candidate. You can also create a situation where the candidate will be under stress and will not interact as freely as he or she would with an easier questioning approach. This also may create a confrontation situation which could inhibit the flow of information. Therefore, to probe in depth effectively you must be careful not to subject the candidate to any indignities. You must exercise extreme tact and must carefully modulate your voice, using the proper inflection and tone you must create an atmosphere that leads the applicant to believe that you are very much interested in the subject matter that you are discussing, and furthermore, that your questions are completely job related and are objective in nature and relevant to assessing the candidate in a fair and impartial manner.

To help to prepare you to pursue subject matter by in-depth questioning, the following sample questions have been prepared to enable you to appreciate more freely the value of following through in each subject area. I have broken the questions into four fairly common areas: work pattern, educational and social pattern, personality, and ambitions. You should, however, develop your own sets of questions initially for your own particular interview situation. You will find as you become more adept in the interview process that in-depth questioning patterns will become second nature to you. You will also discover that you can probe in depth without creating undue stress or without coming across as if you are conducting an interrogation. The amount of information that you will gather will more than offset any adverse effects, if handled properly. The thing to bear in mind is that your major focus during the interview is to dig out the facts objectively and effectively. Here are the questions mentioned earlier.

Work patterns

- *Tell me about* your work history.
  How did you happen to get the job?
  I'd be interested in knowing the kinds of work you did.
  Would you explain your reason (s) for leaving?

- *Tell me more about* what you found disappointing or frustrating in your work.
  Would you explain why?

- *Would you tell me about* what criticism was made of your work by your employers?
  I'm not certain I understand what kind of criticism.
  To what do you attribute the criticism?

- *I'd be interested in knowing,* what is most important to you in a job?
  Would you explain what you care least about in a job?
  What do you mean by that?

- *Tell me about* your usual reaction when called down by a superior for doing something wrong.

- If you were in a position to make changes on your previous jobs, *tell me about* what you would have done.
  Would you explain that in more detail?

- *How do you feel about* relocating and travel away from home?
  Perhaps you could clarify . . .when would you be able to relocate?

Educational and social pattern

• *Tell me about* your scholastic performance in college. In other schools.

What was there about the extracurricular activities you participated in *that appealed to you,* and what offices did you hold in high school? In college?

• *Has there been an opportunity for you to* earn a portion of your educational expenses?

What prompted your decision to do that?

• *Would you tell me about* the experience during your school days that stands out as meaning the most to you?

To what do you attribute the importance of that experience?

• *Would you tell me about* how old you were when you earned your first money on a steady job?

How did you happen to do that?

• *Tell me about* your participation in outside activities.

Personality

• *Would you tell me about* what you believe to be your strong points as a person?

What do you mean by that?

• *I'd be interested in knowing* what you believe to be your weak points as a person.

What do you mean by that?

• *Would you tell me about* qualities you admire in other people?

Perhaps you could clarify why you admire these qualities.

• *Tell me about* what irritates or displeases you most in other people.

- *I'd be interested in knowing about* the last incident that made you angry.
Would you explain what you did about it?

Ambitions

- *I'd be interested in knowing* what position you want to hold several years from now.
Would you tell me about why you believe you will be qualified for that position?

- *I'm not certain I understand* your plans to make yourself qualified.

- *Tell me about* the reputation you like to enjoy as an employee.
What do you mean by that?

- *What prompted your decision to* apply for this job with our company?

- *Would you explain* why you feel we should hire you?

CHAPTER NINE

Evaluating data and articulating the results

The primary purpose of conducting an interview is to reach a conclusion as to whether or not you will hire a candidate. To reach that conclusion you need to keep an open mind as long as possible. As you question the candidate, listen to his or her responses, and take notes, you will find yourself piling up information on the negative side and on the positive side. Rarely will the information be purely positive or purely negative. Almost always you will have to make a judgment that places the information in one category or the other.

To further complicate the situation, you may have to explain to others involved in the hiring process, such as your supervisor, why you judged one way or the other. In many cases, you will find it practically impossible to articulate the relative importance of all the various factors that you will have unearthed during the interview. The sum total of them, however, may add up to what may be described as that "old gut feeling" or, to be more polite, that "back of the neck feeling" that something about the candidate isn't exactly as it should be. Hence, a significant problem in the interview process is that of data evaluation and interpretation.

To solve this problem effectively and efficiently you

must be able to do three things. First, you should pinpoint exactly what you are looking for in nouns, verbs, and adjectives. In other words, you have to describe the criteria thoroughly and accurately. Second, after you have described the criteria, you must be able to ask relevant questions during the interview that will allow you to test whether or not the applicant meets the criteria you have set forth. Third, you must be able to determine how close or how far the applicant comes to meeting the criteria, and you must be able to describe those variances in words.

There is an effective way to do this. As you recall in Chapter Two, in the section dealing with the development of a selection strategy, we talked about establishing a candidate's profile with words that described the various personal characteristics of the person we were seeking. Let's take that process one step further. By so doing, we can tie the selection strategy, the interview, and the interpretation of the data gathered into one smooth, synchronized process. All that is required is to take a selection factor, break it down into two fundamental parts, and expand each part so the selection factor not only gains in clarity and precision of definition but also meshes firmly as an integral part of the interview. Here is how it works.

The method consists of taking a selection factor and breaking it into two parts. The first part consists of defining the selection factor in terms of its elements. The second part consists of a listing of clues to search for as the applicant talks. If the clues are present, then you can not only substantiate your evaluation but you can also articulate your findings much more effectively.

For example, suppose one of the selection factors is mental effectiveness. Using the above method you would break that selection factor down into two parts. The first part would consist of a definition of the selection factor in terms of its key elements. The second part would pinpoint and expand on the meaning of the selection factor. It would look like this.

Mental effectiveness

Mental effectiveness as a selection factor means how the candidate uses his or her mental abilities. It encompasses such things as:

- ability to reason

- ability to think logically

- ability to express ideas precisely

- ability to anticipate, to look ahead, or to plan well

- ability to express ideas well

- ability to get at the central issue in a problem quickly

- ability to spot the differences between important and unimportant matters

- tendency to be mentally alert, curious, and inquisitive rather than a tendency to be sluggish, narrow in interests, or incurious

- capacity to learn from previous experience and to learn material quickly.

The second part consists of a list of indications or clues that you would listen for as the candidate talks. It also provides you with a track to run on as you question and evaluate the applicant against the selection factor. Some of the indications of mental effectiveness would be:

- Is the candidate precise or fuzzy in remembering dates, places, names?

- Does the candidate quickly understand your question? Try a complex question, such as "What are the important things to look for in a job?" How does the candidate handle it? Can the candidate sort out the important from the unimportant things to look for in a job?

• Does it take a long time for the candidate to express an idea?

• Does the candidate organize his or her answers to complex questions? For example, does the candidate say, "Well, there are three things that I look for in a job: one . . ., two . . ., three . . ."

• Does the candidate ask you questions that are sharp and precise? Is he or she with you as you talk together, or passive and mentally unalert?

• Can the candidate back up a general statement, such as "I like selling because I like people," with some specifics, or when you ask for a general statement is it followed up with more vague generalizations? Challenge the candidate to explain some generalization and see whether it is just a run-of-the-mill, platitudinous statement that doesn't represent much thinking or whether it is a carefully thought-through conviction.

• How well can the candidate explain something? For example, if the candidate mentions a process, a product, a situation that you know nothing or little about, ask the candidate to tell you about it. Be genuinely interested, and watch whether words are used well in explaining clearly and precisely what he or she is talking about.

• Pick out some general statement that has been made ("The Republicans have got a fight on their hands in this campaign," or "I like your corporation because it's a progressive company," or "I prefer selling to manufacturing because in selling you deal with people"). Ask the candidate to elaborate, to explain why he or she said that; even be a little skeptical as to the truth of the statement. In short, dig into the caliber of thinking that has gone into these generalizations.

By using this two-step approach you gain an effective method whereby you can evaluate the candidate more precisely against the selection criteria. You also can articulate how well or how poorly the candidate met the criteria simply by comparing the candidate's responses to the indicators. For example, if it turned out that the candidate was mentally effective, you could articulate that judgment by simply stating, "The candidate was able to reason; demonstrate an ability to think logically; was able to express ideas precisely," and so forth.

The beauty of this method is that it is a catalyst for the entire interview process. It provides the grease to make everything work! It promotes careful thought in developing precise selection criteria. It gives the interviewer a framework within which questions can be easily formulated. It provides a systematic approach for evaluative judgments.

It supplies nouns, verbs, and adjectives that can be used to articulate the pros and cons of the candidate. Overall it is an excellent method to use, and I guarantee it will work for you.

In the course of interviewing over the past years I have developed a set of selection factors that apply to almost every interview situation. I include them here for your information and potential application. In your own particular situation you may have to develop your own set of selection factors. If so, I recommend this two-step method very strongly for the reasons I have already stated. I have already covered mental effectiveness. Some additional selection factors that I use and find to be very effective in evaluating candidates follow.

Character and personality

In the category of character and personality, you are asked to make judgments about what kind of person this is; you are dealing entirely with intangible matters and minimal cues.

Character may be viewed more as a matter of what a person's principles are, what he or she thinks is right and wrong; *personality* is more a matter of whether he or she is interesting or dull, weak or strong, rigid and unyielding, or friendly and amiable, mature or immature, tense or relaxed, and so forth. In short, I could oversimplify by saying character is whether a person is a "good person" or a "bad person," while personality, having no moral judgment in it, is a question of whether the person is effective or ineffective in social impact.

Some indicators of character and personality are:

• What are the candidate's values? (For example, if you ask, "Why do you want to work for this particular company?" what does the answer show as to values? Money? Challenge? Opportunity? Security?)

• Is the candidate grown up, mature, able to act his or her age? Indications of immaturity include (you can add many more) self-pity, a big "I," poor perspective on some disappointment or difficulty that has occurred in the past, excessive impulsiveness, and so forth. Indications of maturity include a quiet sureness about career goals or other personal goals; a broad perspective on the ups and downs of daily living; good self-honesty; a tendency to look at reality squarely; a capacity to be enthusiastic without overtones of being an eager beaver; and so on.

• How tense is the candidate? For example, does he or she fidget and squirm, tap fingers, swing feet, blush easily, frown a lot, squint, or in general show outward signs of excessive inner agitation? Sit too still or tensed in the sense of being rigid? Is his or her voice modulated or monotonous? What is the overall body language?

• Is the candidate a person of convictions and quiet beliefs or one who is highly prejudiced and emotional about what he or she thinks?

• Look at the feeling tone to the candidate's personality: does the candidate make noises like a person who enjoys life? Is the candidate enthusiastic? Interested? Alive? Is there warmth and positiveness of feeling to the comments, or is he or she negative or excessively detached or "dead" in feeling? Can the candidate smile? Laugh with you?

• How big is the world that the candidate lives in? For example, is his or her life bounded by the job, family, physical being and by those other things that have a direct effect? Or does the candidate have outside interests—belonging to groups and organizations, giving time in church, scout activities, professional groups, neighborhood gatherings? Is the candidate genuinely concerned about the state of American business or about big issues such as inflation, the security of the free enterprise system, and so forth?

Skill in human relations

In considering the selection factors of skill in human relations, the concern is with how the candidate relates to other people, that is, what are his or her skills and also attitudes toward others, understandings, personal warmth, and so forth? In other words this category encompasses all the things in the person that bear on how he or she gets along with people.

Some indicators of skill in human relations are:

• Do you like him or her as a person? If not, can you put your finger on what causes your dislike?

• Does the candidate have a history of good social relations? Does he or she have several close friends? Does he or she obviously enjoy his or her family relations? Does the candidate have a history of leadership activities, such as president of class, chairperson of committees, motivator in neighborhood activities?

• Does the candidate have a sense of humor? Is it wholesome and comfortable or does he or she wisecrack a lot?

• How well does he or she seem to understand people? For example, when the candidate has talked about his or her boss, or a colleague, or a friend, can he or she cite specific characteristics that the person has? Can he or she analyze behavior? Is he or she self-assertive and why? Try objecting to something the candidate has said. Can he or she good humoredly stick to his or her guns? Does the candidate quietly control you? Does the candidate argue quickly and differ with you tactfully? Does he or she go after you with some penetrating questions? For example, ask him or her, "What are two or three basic things about the company that I can tell you?" Does the candidate make you perform nicely for him or her?

Understanding of self and others

In this category, the person's view of self and of others is the focus of your attention. You are trying to understand how much insight into self and others the person has. Insight is the capacity to see into, literally; to look behind the obvious and overt behavior. Insight, particularly self-insight, is a most difficult capacity to analyze.

Here are two examples of insight:

• A person and three companions are dining in a public restaurant. The person is all involved in relating an experience he or she has just been through, and gradually he or she talks louder and louder and longer and longer. The person's companions are politely interested at first, then they begin covertly to glance at each other and at the people at nearby tables to see how others are reacting to the person's loud talking; they diddle with their food; no one, although they all want to, definitely shushes the person. Suddenly, the person realizes how long and loudly he or she has been talking. He or she gets insight. The person sees himself or herself, in short, as others do.

• A person is a perfectionist and knows it. He or she gets along fine when he or she is the only one affected by his or her perfectionism; for instance, he or she has an impeccable lawn at home, works at it constantly, and never allows a weed to get started. But at the office, the perfectionism gets the person into constant trouble because he or she demands perfection of his or her subordinates—and they aren't about to be so perfect. He or she criticizes freely, gets mad, never finds any good in anything, and creates tension wherever he or she goes. Let's say that through a fortunate chain of circumstances he or she suddenly realizes that he or she is his or her own worst critic, and that a person that can't accept his or her own human frailties in reality hates himself or herself, and that this is what causes his or her perfectionism and driving demand of others. This "sudden realization" is insight.

In interviewing applicants, you will want to get some insights into the applicant's capacity to "see self as others see you" and into his or her capacity to see into why others feel and act as they do.

You might ask the applicant, "Would you describe your best boss for me?" If he or she does and then maybe says "Of course, I need a boss who can keep ahead of me, keep me challenged, because I bore easily," the applicant is expressing self-understanding, and the interviewer's job then is to check it out. Is this person right in his or her self-view? If so, the person has some self-insight.

The applicant might ask you, "Is this the information you want?" or "Do you want more detail than I've given you?" or he or she might indicate in other ways sharp awareness of your inner feelings, wishes, and attitudes. This is the applicant's social insight.

Supervisory ability

In evaluating supervisory ability, try to make judgments on the applicant's ability to handle authority over others. Obviously, the previous categories—mental effectiveness, character and personality, relations with others, and insight—bear heavily on supervisory ability.

The interviewer may look for those characteristics of the applicant as a supervisor that go beyond the former categories:

- Is the applicant a "take charge" kind of person?

- Is the applicant a person who plans his or her life well to reach planned goals?

- Is the applicant capable of stimulating others to work hard?

- Does the applicant have a contagious enthusiasm?

- Is the applicant a natural leader?

In other words, supervisory ability is really not a single, special ability; it is, rather, the total impact of the applicant if he or she were in charge of a group, small or large.

Indicators of supervisory ability are:

- In school and previous work situations, has the applicant had supervisory jobs—chairperson, president, leader? As he or she tells you about these jobs, does the person seem to have been "on top" of the situation?

- When given a chance to, in your interview with the candidate, does he or she move in and take charge of you? For example, by asking questions, by directing the course of the conversation, or by assuming responsibility for the shape of things?

- As the applicant talks with you about his or her "best boss" or "worst boss," does he or she seem to have a feeling for the boss's responsibilities? If critical, are the criticisms indicative of a good perception on the applicant's part of the job of a supervisor?

- If you should choose to disagree with the applicant, does he or she suddenly fold up? Or can the person argue with you (tactfully, of course)? Is he or she overly solicitous, amenable? Is the person overly rigid, insistent on his or her exact point of view?

- What does the person do with spare time that indicates a "take charge" kind of person? For example, do projects around the house get finished? Has the applicant organized a neighborhood committee or run a church social, Sunday School, PTA, lodge, political group?

Selling or service ability

Like the category of supervisory ability, selling or service ability is not a single and distinct ability. It involves, rather, a judgment on the pattern of the person's mental effectiveness, character and personality, relations with others, insight, appearance, and so on.

- Is the applicant sufficiently intelligent to learn the entire product line, to properly analyze customer problems, to present a well-organized proposal, to close the sale, and to profit by each subsequent experience?

- Is the applicant of good character and personality? Would he or she gain customer confidence? Could the candidate be trusted to operate effectively and in a polite manner with a minimum of supervision? Has the candidate sufficient drive and persistence? Confidence? Self-control? Stability of purpose? Is the person a self-starter? Independent? Enthusiastic?

- Is the candidate skillful at human relations? Sense of humor? Personal warmth? Is he or she self-assertive? Tactful?

- Does the applicant have sufficient insight to project his or her personality into a customer's situation? Can he or she appreciate the customer's problem? Choose the best course for overcoming the customer's reservations?

- Is he or she neat? Poised? Courteous? Does he or she have pleasing mannerisms?

Indicators of selling ability are:

- Convincing conversationalist? Precise? Able to recall details readily? Alert? Capable of deep, as opposed to superficial, conversation?

114

• Has the applicant demonstrated an ability to over-come adversity without self-pity? Placed business before pleasure? Does educational and professional back-ground reflect clarity of goals and persistence toward achievement? Has it been shown that he or she is in command of his or her own ship, or has the applicant simply sailed with the current? Is the applicant anxious for an opportunity to prove himself or herself, or is the applicant looking for security? Has it been indicated that the applicant habitually gives work that extra effort so essential to sales leadership?

• Does he or she speak well of others? Is he or she polite and tactful in defending a position or in seeking conversational leadership? Does the applicant have and maintain close friendships? Do you enjoy being with the applicant?

• Does the applicant describe people in depth, rather than in terms of their most overt characteristics? Has the applicant analyzed his or her own self realistically?

• Does the applicant appear and act as if healthy? Energetic?

• Has the applicant studied subjects related to the work he or she is seeking? Does the career show income growth indicative of having performed well?

• Has the applicant exhibited sound personal financial management? Does the applicant have sufficient eco-nomic need to provide strong motivation?

• Is the applicant "things" or "people" oriented in spare time?

General impact

As was the case with the two previous categories, general impact is a multifactor category calling for a general state-ment about your reaction to the applicant as a person. Does the applicant inspire you or leave you cold? Is the applicant interesting or dull? Does the applicant have personal warmth and charm? In short, does the applicant tend to attract or repel you?

Some indicators relating to impact are:

• Is the applicant neat? Robust? Does he or she have good posture? Good facial expression?

• Is the applicant tactful? Courteous? Confident? Warm? Enthusiastic? Cheerful? Optimistic? Animated? Humorous?

• Does the applicant have good pronunciation? Enunciation? Vocabulary? Grammar? Does the applicant express himself or herself freely? With clarity? In an organized manner?

• Does the applicant have good educational and professional backgrounds?

• Has the applicant exhibited mental effectiveness? Good character and personality? Skill in human relations? Insights?

• In short, beginning with your initial contact did you immediately sense that this person is exceptional and likely to be hired?

The above selection factors are but a small sample of what can be done in the way of focusing on precise meaningful criteria that can greatly increase your interviewing effectiveness when used to full advantage.

The two-step process combining "meaning of the selection factor" with "some indicators of the selection factor" can be applied to virtually any selection factors or criteria.

Once you establish the key word or words for your base criteria, it is relatively easy to expand that into a "meaning" part and an "indicator" part. When you are able to do that, you will be well on your way toward increasing your interviewing skills dramatically.

CHAPTER TEN

Making the decision

Following the hiring sequence you have screened the applicant, analyzed test results (where applicable), and gathered information during the interview. You, and the other members of the interviewing team, have accumulated a great deal of information about the applicant. Now you must sort through that information and decide whether or not to extend an offer of employment.

In making that judgment, you must be aware of and be able to recognize how much of your information is factual and how much of it consists of inferences.

Fact versus inference

In any unfamiliar situation that you approach, such as interviewing an applicant, you may gather information that may be factual or may consist to a degree of inferences. Whether or not you have facts or inferences depends on how much subjectivity is present in your interpretation versus how much objectivity or evidence is present in the information. If there is a lot of objectivity present and there is reality present, then your information is factual. It can be observed, it is certain, and it can be proven. You would stake your reputation on it. If, however, on the other hand, there is a lot of subjectivity or "you" present in the information, then it is an inference. It was not or cannot be observed, it is not certain, it cannot be proven. You would not stake your reputation on it.

In your evaluation of the applicant you should aim at making all judgments "statements of fact." You should give the most weight to the information that is the most factual and objective and less to that information that is subjective.

The significance of the data

It must be stressed that any data obtained on a candidate are essentially meaningless unless we know what the data mean, that is, the significance of the data in terms of the likelihood of the candidate to succeed or to fail on the job in your company. Furthermore, the data must be interpreted within the framework of the specific applicant you are seeking in terms of your selection strategy. The data on the applicant must also be compared with that on the successful, effective person who is already in your employ.

Sources of error

One of the major sources of error in judging others is that we allow our personal biases to influence our judgments. It is only human nature to make certain judgments about applicants even though our total exposure to them has been only for a short time during an interview. Any general impressions and any subjective judgments that you make must be recognized as such so they will only play a very minor part in your final decision. As an interviewer, you must be aware of human tendencies to ensure that your own personal biases do not have an undue influence on the hiring decision. There are a number of errors that interviewers are prone to make. You should be alert to these so you can avoid them in your assessment of others.

The first impression

All too often, interviewers let their first impression of an applicant influence not only the course of the interview but also the evaluation of the candidate as well. In some cases, interviewers will reach a conclusion during the first minutes of an hour interview. Frequently, those judgments are based on superficial characteristics that are unrelated to success on the job. A major problem with judgments based on initial impressions is that they are often based on information that is not related to the selection standards. For example, firmness of handshake, dress or hairstyle. Once you form an initial impression you will find yourself selectively seeking out information that is consistent with your initial impression. If you place too much importance on the initial or first impression that the applicant makes on you, then all too often you will have made your decision that the person is right or wrong for the job, and the rest of the interview will be spent trying to prove that your judgment was correct rather than maintaining an open mind.

Favorable versus unfavorable information

Frequently, interviewers who turn up 99 percent favorable items and one unfavorable item will give a disproportionate weight to the one unfavorable item. This suggests that negative information is much more influential than favorable information. If the interviewer concentrates on highlights, disqualifying all negative evidence, it is highly unlikely that the candidate will be evaluated properly. This course of error must be recognized so the proper weight can be given to both positive and negative data.

The halo effect

The halo effect is one of the most common and critical errors that is made in assessing others. If the interviewer permits one trait, favorable or unfavorable, to influence his or her thinking, then that interviewer's judgment will suffer from the halo effect. For example, the candidate who makes a good appearance is often presumed to be good in all other areas as well. A good assessment of that person would be that he or she makes a good appearance and nothing more. Even though many traits and abilities are often related to other characteristics and skills, each one should be evaluated on its own merits. One trait should not influence our impressions in other areas.

Forgetting

In assessing others we conveniently forget those items that run contrary to our final decision. If we are positive about a candidate, we somehow manage to forget much of the unfavorable data. The sharp assessor generally records information during the interview so all data, favorable and unfavorable, is considered in the final decision.

Hiring in one's own image

It is very human to respond more favorably to applicants whose background is similar to your own. Whenever an interviewer's educational, economic, ethnic, or geographic experiences are similar to the applicant's, then generally that applicant would score better in the final assessment.

Oversimplification

While it is tempting to express complicated behavioral traits in simple terms, it can often lead to false assumptions or conclusions. In assessing others you must view the data in their entirety. For example, it is not enough to say that a candidate is aggressive. The trait of aggressiveness is far too complex to be described in one word. On one side of the coin, an aggressive person can be forceful, dynamic, tough-minded, and self-confident. On the other side, that same person can be inflexible, tactless, insensitive to others, and can have a tendency to be too blunt or direct. Even though it is tempting to express complicated behavioral traits in simple terms, it is naive to do so. You will find yourself more often wrong than right.

Projection

This error is made when you attribute your own feelings or ideas to another person. It may influence your judgment either negatively or positively depending on how you view the candidate.

If, for example, you view the candidate as a younger version of yourself in that he or she reminds you very much of yourself when you were starting with the firm, then you may be susceptible to projection. Even though the applicant may not have the same experience and educational background as yourself, you may find yourself attributing your own feelings and values to the candidate. The candidate's real values and feelings may be totally different from yours, hence a source of error in your judgment.

False values

These are criteria that are set up either consciously or unconsciously, outside the selection criteria. Frequently, the interviewer is unaware of them. For example, an interviewer may unjustifiably feel that no person can succeed in a job unless he or she is attractive or is a graduate of a certain school. If the interviewer persists in using non-job-related criteria he or she will fail to select the most effective candidate.

Verbal facility

Many people fall into the trap of ascribing positive qualities to others solely on the basis of verbal facility. One may include this as a part of the "halo effect" if it were not for the great significance it has in the judgment process. It must be clearly recognized that skill as a speaker does not automatically stand a person's total ability in good stead. If I had to single out a universal fault that exists in judging others I would have to point the finger at the "articulate" candidate. If you are overly impressed with a good talker and underimpressed by one of modest verbal facility, then you are a prime candidate to make an error in judgment on this one. Be on guard against the smooth talker.

To summarize, you can greatly enhance and increase your chances of making sound employment decisions if you rely on factual and objective data and less on subjective judgment. Furthermore, if you understand and recognize the kinds of errors that can be made in the assessment process, then you will be less prone to make them.

As a final comment, the various tools that are brought to bear in the selection process will no doubt uncover a number of imperfections and weaknesses in the applicant. If this were not the case, then there would be something wrong with the selection process. This unfavorable information must be weighed with the favorable information and a balanced judgment must be made. Nobody is perfect. If we seek only perfection, we may go for long periods with unfilled jobs.

CHAPTER ELEVEN

Listening: a critical requirement

During the course of the interview, the applicant will be doing most of the talking, and you will be doing most of the listening. This is good and desirable, providing you are a good listener. Good listening is one of the important skills that you will need if you aspire to become an effective interviewer. It will not do you any good to extract data successfully from a candidate if you do not hear the data when they are put forth. Far too much information is lost as a result of poor listening. To be a good listener you must work hard at it. In addition to all the other skills and techniques that are brought to bear during the interview, the skill of good listening is a critical requirement that if not met renders all your other skills useless.

Many interviewers lose out because they are poor listeners. I recall one fellow who seemed to think that everything the candidate said called for relating his own personal experiences, usually interjected before the candidate could finish a sentence. "I work at American Metals and I . . .," said the candidate. "Oh," interrupted the interviewer, "my brother worked there for three years." "Yes," said the candidate, "and I worked in the Accounting Department."

"My brother left American Metals to move out West, he wanted a warmer climate."

Needless to say, this interviewer is not going to get much useable information from the candidate. At the end of the interview the candidate would probably know more about the interviewer than vice versa.

Let me give you some ideas on listening. Research has shown that although everyone listens, most of us listen ineffectively. If we understand what the essential elements are that make some people good listeners and others poor listeners, then we can learn how to increase our ability to identify and to retain the critical content of what we hear.

Active listening

To be a good, active listener, several components must be recognized and grasped. To begin with, one must prepare to listen. This is accomplished by recalling everything you know that relates to what you are about to hear. Let's see how this process works.

Preparation

Imagine that you are about to hear a candidate describe his or her formal educational background. You would go over in your mind everything you know about formal education. Starting out with grade school, you would probably think "Oh, yes, let me see, I know that grade school is usually eight years, you get promoted each year or you stay back. High school is generally four years; you prepare for a vocation, or you take a college preparatory program; you play high school sports and/or participate in extracurricular activities; you take courses in language, math, social studies, history, and so on; you get passing grades or failing grades; you graduate, perhaps with honors; one graduate gets to be valedictorian. College involves going to a 'good' school, passing or failing courses, participating in extracurricular activities, holding office in a club or organization, electing a major field of study, pursuing a degree, changing your major or changing schools, graduating, achieving honors. . . . I know about formal education."

As you warm up this way for listening to what the speaker is about to say you are prepared to look for the similarities or differences to what you already know compared with what you are about to hear. This preparation consists of a systematic comparison of what you already know to what you are about to hear. You prepare by asking yourself, "What do I already know?" Then you ask yourself about the similarities that exist between what you already know and what you've just heard. You then focus on the advantages or disadvantages of the similarities. At the same time you ask yourself about the differences that exist between what you already know and what you've heard and, likewise, you focus on the advantages or disadvantages of those differences.

Summarizing what you hear

After you prepare yourself for listening and you engage in interactive listening, you must be able to summarize, in your mind, what the speaker has said. This can be accomplished by recognizing the speaker's main points and the supporting points that are used to embellish the main points.

For example, the speaker may say, "The reason I left my last job was for lack of opportunity." The main point is "lack of opportunity." The speaker may then support that point by saying, "The company very rarely promotes from within, and even if they did, I would have to wait for my boss to move up or out. Also, the company's growth has slowed down and promotional opportunities are rare."

The main point is "lack of opportunity," the supporting points are "rarely promotes from within," "wait for boss to move," "company's growth has slowed." To listen effectively, you must be able to identify the main points and the supporting points while you are listening. By doing so, you will retain more of the statement.

To summarize what you hear effectively, it is extremely helpful to note only those words or phrases that are important in identifying the main points and the supporting points. These words can be called "keywords" since they provide the key to what the speaker is trying to get across. For example, in the statement "I desire a position with your company so I can become a manager in a few years," the key word is "become". If you want a manager right away you may reject the candidate that does not expect to start the job as a manager. Recognition of the key word "become" will assist you in listening to the speaker's main point which is "become a manager."

In supporting the main point, the speaker may say, "I have always admired your company, and I want to become a part of its management team. Although I do not have previous management experience, I have an excellent academic background, and I am a fast learner." Here the key words are "become a manager", "do not have previous experience". They are used to support the main point that the candidate wants to "become a manager."

As the speaker talks, and as you use key words to identify the main and supporting points, you must weight them as being in favor for or against the speaker. This can be accomplished by grouping the points into categories such as the one we already discussed, namely similarities/differences and other categories such as advantages/disadvantages and causes/effects.

You would ask yourself in the above situation, "How am I, the listener, similar or different from the candidate in terms of the requirements of the job?" Is it an advantage or disadvantage for the candidate to want to become a manager at a future date? What caused the candidate to lack management experience, and what is the effect of that shortcoming? As you categorize the main and supporting points and as you compare them to your own situation, you are well on your way to becoming a good interactive listener. You are now in a position to ask the speaker to clarify statements for you or to elaborate on them. Furthermore, you can also confirm your understanding of any point that isn't clear.

Blocks to effective listening

The final key to good listening is to be able to overcome any blocks or obstacles that may keep you from listening effectively. These can be environmental factors such as sights and sounds that distract your attention. Your personal opinions or biases may prevent you from listening to the speaker's entire message. Oftentimes accents, improper grammar, or slang will force your attention to the structure rather than to the content and meaning. Probably the most flagrant block to effective listening is that of selective listening. The selective listener allows himself or herself to hear only what he or she wants to hear and to tune out everything else. It sometimes happens that the listener may start out the day as a good interactive effective listener. However, the interviewer may have a heavy schedule, and as the day wears on, he or she finds that he or she is suffering from an information overload and that he or she starts to lose the concentration necessary to listen effectively. Suddenly, it dawns on you that you have tuned out and you are only occasionally hearing what the speaker has been saying. You have set up a block and have been selectively listening to only part of the speaker's words. To get back your effectiveness you will have to bear down with your powers of concentration, otherwise call it a day since you will have lost your effectiveness and your ability to absorb the data.

Some do's and don't's on listening

In addition to the above advice, here are some do's and don't's when it comes to listening:

- Recognize that you think about four times as fast as the person can talk. This naturally gives your brain excess time to think. Don't use that excess time to turn your thoughts elsewhere. If you do, you will find yourself dividing your attention between listening to the speaker and listening to yourself. To accomplish your primary task, that of gathering information from the speaker, you must give the speaker your undivided attention.

- Do not let certain words, phrases, or ideas prejudice you against the speaker so you cannot listen objectively to what is being said. If the speaker uses a word incorrectly or mispronounces a word or uses the wrong tense in a sentence, do not dwell on it, but rather let it go. Your task is to listen objectively to the content and not the form. (The form may well be important, but you can file it away in the back of your mind as a separate issue to be dealt with after the interview. Possibly in the evaluation stage.)

- If you are annoyed or irritated by what has been said, do not interrupt the speaker to try to straighten it out. Furthermore, do not dwell on it in your own mind as it will distract you from listening.

- If the speaker says something that you do not understand, do not tune out, especially if you feel that it will take too much time and effort to understand.

- Do not deliberately turn your thoughts to other subjects if you believe that the speaker has nothing interesting to say. This is a natural result of boredom. Once you feel that the speaker is dull or uninteresting, you invariably occupy your mind with thoughts that are more interesting to you. During the interview, you must force yourself to listen. A method that I have found useful in dealing with this problem is to try to gauge just how boring the person can really be. It may sound a bit off the wall, but I have found that by playing the game "How Big a Bore Have I Here?", it has helped me to listen to the person, to the bitter end of the interview. Naturally, my postinterview evaluation took that observation into consideration.

• Do not let a person's appearance or speech pattern influence you into thinking that the candidate may not have anything worthwhile to say. So the candidate is not attired in a smart up-to-date, tasteful outfit but rather in seedy, tasteless, outmoded garb. As much as you want to tune the person out, don't do it. You never know what or who is hiding beneath that garb. The only way you're going to find out is by listening.

• Finally, do not pretend to be listening if you're not. Pay attention!

Remember, good listening is essential in an interview and, furthermore, because of human nature, most people like good listeners. It's a fact. People prefer to have people listen to them much more than they prefer to listen themselves. In the interview situation, the ability to be a good, interactive listener is the key to being effective.

CHAPTER TWELVE

Testing applicants

The use of tests in the employment process has greatly decreased since 1968. It was in late 1968 that the Federal Employment Opportunity Commission and the Office of Federal Contract Compliance started to require companies having government contracts to validate their employment tests. The requirement for validation meant that employers using tests for screening applicants had to prove that candidates who scored high on a given test would do better than those who scored low. Hence, some measure of job performance became necessary. Some typical measures of job performance are production, quantity or quality, costs, absenteeism, labor turnover, and performance ratings by supervisors. If the company proved that their tests would allow them to predict that the performance of the high scorers was at least 20 percent above that of the low scorers, then it could be shown to the government that the test was a valid indicator or predictor of success on the job.

Validating employment tests

It was not very difficult to validate tests that were designed to rate employees on easily measured tasks, such as typing or steno or other manual skills. It was, however, somewhat more difficult to validate tests that measured qualities such as personality or motivation, intelligence or management potential, or a host of other behavior criteria. As a result, many companies abandoned their testing programs that were used to screen professional applicants.

The demise of testing is somewhat unfortunate since the proper use of tests can serve as an important tool in the selection process. Years of research have undeniably pointed to the value of tests in making an accurate prediction on a person's future performance.

"Okay," you may say, "I believe that tests can be a valuable aid in the interview and selection process, but how do I get around the validation requirements of the federal government?"

Simple; you can validate practically any test without too much effort, and I'll show you how in a moment. First of all, before we get into validation in detail, let's take a moment and talk about tests in general. "What," one may ask, "is a test, and what difference does it make if a person can solve a paper-and-pencil exercise, especially if he or she doesn't have to do that on the job?"

Well, okay, those are fair questions. First of all, a test is a measuring tool that allows us to see a small slice of an applicant's characteristics, taken under uniform and standardized conditions. If that slice is selected properly so as to predict a broad area of the job, then it can be shown that those properly selected test items will be able to predict performance in a real-life situation. What is being sought is a way of determining whether an applicant will be a high or low producer. Years of research have proven beyond a shadow of a doubt that tests can be of value in helping to make that prediction.

An important feature of tests is that they can be given under relatively constant conditions. This proves to be an advantage when comparing the performance of different applicants because it decreases the number of variables present and permits a more direct measurement which is generally more accurate and consistent from one candidate to the next.

If we accept the fact that people differ, then we must try to discover the candidate whose qualifiactions best match the requirements of the job. Determining the degree of differences among persons may be easy or may prove difficult depending on the qualifications needed.

It's obvious that people differ in appearance. And it's also obvious that people differ in thier educational level and past experience. These differences are easy to determine from the candidate's résumé and application and during the interview.

Differences in basic abilities, interests, and values are not so obvious and they are hard to get at during an interview or by reading the person's résumé or application. It is in these areas that tests can make the greatest contribution by providing an accurate and efficient means of measuring these important characteristics.

The different tests that are used to measure behavior generally can be grouped into several major categories such as:

- *aptitude tests,* which predict a person's ability to learn new tasks, such as electronics or mechancial repair

- *achievement tests,* which measure the person's level of learning based on past education—they measure the level of performance that resulted from past study

- *general ability tests,* which measure the thinking or learning abilities that provide an indication of general intelligence

- *special ability tests,* which measure specific abilities or areas of performance, for example, verbal abilities, numerical reasoning abilities, and mechanical abilities

- *personality tests,* which center on a person's social adjustment and character traits, such as responsibility, maturity and cooperativeness

- *biographical inventories,* which include items that record a person's background and experiences, generally items about a person's education, jobs, military experience, and so forth; they may also include items on a person's hobbies, interests, and attitudes.

Although tests can definitely improve your chances of hiring the right person, they do have some limitations. They are definitely not a magic potion that will guarantee you 100 percent results. Not only will tests not work in every situation but, when they do work, they will not yield perfect results. In addition, no one test or battery of tests can measure all the factors you should consider when making your hiring decision.

With these thoughts in mind, let's take a look at three relatively easy ways to validate employment tests. You can validate employment tests based on your present employees, based on applicants, or by correlation.

Validation based
on present employees

Rank eight or more present employees according to one or more job criteria. Divide them into two equal groups: one group above average and the other below average. Have both groups take the test that you are considering using. Score each test and compute the average test score of each group. If the average of the high group is at least 20 percent higher than the low group, then you have proof that the test is valid.

Administer the test to all applicants, but do not use the test scores in the hiring process. That is, do not let the hiring managers see the test results. After three months of service obtain a performance rating on each employee. Compare the performance rating with the test results to determine if the test predicted a standing based on whatever criterion was used.

Correlation

If you have fifteen or more cases you can calculate a rank order coefficient of correlation. A computation will allow you to show the correlation between performance against the criteria and the test score. If there is a positive correlation between the person's performance criterion and test rank, such as high performer-high test rank, then you have proof that the test is valid.

There are many formulas for determining coefficients of correlation. The following formula is fairly straightforward and should prove easy to apply.

- *Step one:* List each employee in order of performance criterion with the top performer first.

- *Step two:* Assign appropriate test rank order to each employee.

- *Step three:* Calculate the differences between the criterion rank and the test rank and square the difference. For example, for employee 1, criterion rank equals 11 and test rank equals 13, the difference is 2.

Employee	Criterion Rank	Test Rank	Differences	D^2
A	1	3	2	4
B	2	1	1	1
C	3	5	2	4
D	4	2	2	4
E	5	6	1	1
F	6	4	2	4
G	7	9	2	4
H	8	7	1	1
I	9	11	2	4
J	10	10	0	0
K	11	13	2	4
L	12	8	4	16
M	13	12	1	1
N	14	15	1	1
O	15	14	1	1
				50

A simple formula for computing correlation is:

$$\text{Correlation} = 1.00 - \frac{6 \, (\text{Sum of } D^2)}{n \, (n^2 - 1)}$$

where "n" is the number of cases.

$$= 1.00 - \frac{6 \, (50)}{15 \, (224)}$$

$$= 1.00 - \frac{300}{3340}$$

$$= +.91$$

In the case of our sample, the +.91 is a very high correlation which would indicate that the tests were valid indicators of successful performance against the criterion.

As we saw earlier, there are federal guidelines for validating whether or not a particular test is significantly related to job performance. Although, as an interviewer, you may not get involved in validating tests, I have included this information to assist you in understanding the use of tests and the validation thereof in the hiring process.

CHAPTER THIRTEEN

Tips on fine-tuning your techniques

The following tips will provide you with additional insight to help you to fine-tune your interviewing techniques. Hopefully, they not only will enhance the quality of your interviews but at the same time will help you to save precious time in the process. As a day-to-day practitioner of interviewing people for jobs, I have over the years developed a number of practices that have helped me to become more proficient. I have also explored, pursued, utilized, and discarded a number of concepts that did not work as well as I had imagined they would. In the following paragraphs, I will provide you with some of the things that work, some of the things that don't work, and some of the things that may or may not work, depending on the situation.

Screen, screen, screen

In the interest of time and money, the importance of carefully screening an applicant's papers cannot be emphasized enough. Generally, you will have access to at least two separate documents on each candidate, a résumé and an application. If you have only a résumé, then by all means have the applicant fill out an application. Most application forms contain vital information that is generally left off the résumé. Information such as salary requirements, dates of employment, salary history, names and titles of former and present supervisors, names, addresses and phone numbers of references, military service, and so forth.

The more information you have, the better able you are to screen. There is absolutely nothing to be gained by interviewing a candidate who is seeking a salary considerably more than you are willing to pay. However, I have seen that happen, time and time again. Why? Failure to screen the applicant's papers against the selection criteria.

Even more important is the failure to screen for the less obvious but never-the-less important criteria, such as job progression, reasons for changing jobs, type and quality of past companies, educational track record, and so on.

If you have done a thorough job of screening, you will find yourself champing at the bit to bring in your top candidates on paper. If you don't do a good job at screening, you may find yourself interviewing a high percentage of marginal candidates, whereas they could have been screened out before the interview stage.

The method that I use to screen candidates more thoroughly is to simply ask them to complete whatever papers I feel are needed before inviting them in for an interview. For example, if I run an ad in the paper and receive 80 to 100 responses in the form of résumés, I will screen the résumés down to whatever number meets the criteria. I will be liberal and screen in any résumés that may be on the fence or marginal. I then go back, by letter to each candidate, and request that an application form be filled out "as thoroughly and as completely as possible." On receipt of the completed application, I further screen each candidate. This extra step usually eliminates several more candidates, thus eliminating the need to bring them in for a screening interview. It also, I may add, allows you to make a better judgment at picking the top-ranked candidates. The next step is, of course, to bring in the top candidates. If you have done your paperwork screening thoroughly, you will have cut down the number of interviews and will have increased your chances of finding a suitable candidate quicker.

Don't hire the best of the worst

It sometimes happens that although you do everything right in the recruiting/selection process you end up without a suitable candidate. You face the prospect of starting all over again. That may involve running an ad, screening papers, screening interviews, and so forth. The thought of it sends quivers up your spine. As a result of your first recruiting effort you find yourself with a candidate who doesn't quite meet your criteria; however, he or she came out number one. You feel a strong urge to hire that candidate. Why not? After all, you did run an ad. You did screen and interview. You used up every recruiting source you know. You feel that if you started the campaign again you may do just as poorly. So why not? Why not hire your number one candidate?

The answer is simple. Because the candidate does not meet your criteria. Because you don't want to hire the best of the worst. Because six months from now you may have to do the whole job over again. My advice—don't do it. Go back to the starting point and try again. There are no short cuts to professional recruiting. Leave those shortcuts to the mediocre manager.

Be aware of the "whole person"

Regardless of how precise you are in establishing your selection criteria, you can't describe every single aspect of the ideal candidate. As a result, you will often find during the course of an interview that although the candidate does not meet the "specified" criteria, he or she has certain qualities that transcend the criteria and render the applicant extremely well qualified for success on the job. I call this phenomenon the "whole person" phenomenon that is present in the interview. It is similar to discovering a diamond in the rough. Although the brilliance and fine details are not readily apparent, some cutting and polishing will usually bring out the desired qualities. So it is with people. A candidate may fall short of having the required college degree but may in truth be a brilliant person. Another may fall short in terms of personal appearance but may prove to be beautiful in terms of personality and charm.

As you interview candidates you will be forming an opinion on the whole person, not on individual traits or characteristics. If the individual traits or characteristics fall short individually, but the sum of the parts add up to what you are looking for, then you have found your candidate.

Consider your company's environment

Another factor that must be taken into consideration in the selection process is the company environment and the employee attitudes that the new person will be subjected to. The new employee must be one who will mesh with the organization. Will he or she fit in? Will he or she be accepted? Will he or she thrive in the environment or die on the vine?

Not only does the candidate have to meet the selection standards of the job but also has to meet the general environmental and attitudinal realities that exist in the company. Future problems with the employee can be avoided if these factors are considered. For example, can a successful small businessperson be successful in a giant corporation? Can a person used to individual tasks be successful as part of a team? Can a secretary from a one-person office perform effectively in a large office with over 60 other secretaries? Can a big fish make it in a small pond? Or vice versa. Whatever the situation is in your company, you must take it into account when you hire the new employee. A good test of whether or not you have taken this factor into consideration is to ask yourself if you are hiring the person for the job at hand or whether you are hiring the person for the second and subsequent jobs in the company that he or she will move into through promotion. In other words, as I mentioned earlier, will your new employee thrive or wither in the environment in which you place him or her? If the answer is thrive, then your candidate is suitable for employment.

Beware of the "perfect" candidate

Once in a while you will find yourself with a candidate that is almost too good to be true. He or she meets all your criteria and then some. Your immediate reaction is to make an offer. After all this is the person that you have been diligently seeking or is it? Another factor that must be considered is that of overqualification. If the job does not offer enough challenge, your "perfect" candidate may get restless or bored, and you may find yourself trying once again to fill the position within a short space of time. Insofar as possible you should endeavor to hire the candidate that has to stretch a bit or grow a little to perform the job adequately. It's a tough decision to make, but in the long run it's generally a wiser decision.

Don't be influenced by other interviewers

In a situation in which you have more than one interviewer involved in the process you should strive to eliminate the tendency to influence others or let others influence you—

unduly. You should avoid creating or receiving any preconceived ideas on candidates before or after you interview them.

All too often during the interview process, one interviewer will influence others on the relative merits of a given candidate. Depending on that person's position in the company or on that person's ability to influence others, a shaping process may take place. The interviewers may find themselves accepting one person's viewpoint as a standard for measurement. If the influencer likes a candidate, the other interviewers may find a strong influence at work which will lead them to believe that they too like the candidate. Or even worse, if they didn't like the candidate, they may find themselves going along with the tide in spite of their feelings.

If hiring decisions were made in the thumbs up or thumbs down tradition that the Romans used with their gladiators, then hiring decisions would be a lot more objective. Unfortunately, the power of one to influence others will always exist. If you recognize it at work, you should be able to deal with it even if you can't eliminate it altogether.

Keep notes

Regardless of how good your memory is you will invariably forget things. My advice to you is to keep notes. The written word is far more durable than your memory, and, I might add, far more accurate, especially when you have a heavy interview schedule. If you feel that taking notes may appear awkward or too clinical or too sophomorish, don't! It is a perfectly acceptable activity and is quite commonplace in the interview situation.

To set the candidate's mind at ease about your note-taking activity, all that you have to say is, "As we chat today, I am going to be taking some notes. I'll be writing on your résumé, your application, and on this yellow pad." I have introduced my note-taking activity in that manner hundreds of times, and it has worked smoothly every time. The candidates readily accept it as part and parcel of the process.

Manage your
interview schedule

Don't load yourself up with more interviews than you can do justice to. At the end of the day the applicants will start to blend into one another, and you may find it extremely difficult to focus on the candidates at the end of the schedule.

I recommend not more than four in-depth interviews in any given day. That number has worked well for me in the past and has allowed me to conduct effective interviews from start to finish.

In the case of the shorter screening interviews, twice that number can be handled. Since the screening interview is considerably shorter and does not require as much concentration and effort, one can remain fairly efficient throughout the day.

Don't try to be a hero by conducting marathon interview sessions. There are limits to one's ability to maintain peak efficiency throughout the day. Recognize your limits, and schedule yourself accordingly. In short, manage it to achieve optimum results from the time and energy you invest.

Don't pursue
improper information

Candidates sometimes voluntarily offer information that is improper under the provisions of the equal opportunity laws and executive orders. Without your having to ask any questions whatsoever, the candidate may suddenly reveal that she is married and has three kids. Another reveals that he is in the process of getting divorced. Still another reveals that he is bilingual as a result of being born and raised in Puerto Rico.

Regardless of how the candidate introduces a subject or topic that falls within the realm of improper information, do not pursue it! Simply drop the subject and go onto something else. If you pursue the topic or try to gain clarification, it may result in a discrimination charge against you. It won't matter who introduced the subject. What does matter is that it was discussed, by both parties, during the interview. So beware!

Do not feed the applicant the "right answers"

In a situation where there are two or more interviewers involved in the interview process, you must guard against "feeding" the applicant information that he or she will use to respond to questions from subsequent interviewers. For example, if you indicate that your ideal candidate will possess certain characteristics or certain experiences, then you can be assured that the candidate will strive to display those desired features to the other interviewers.

Also, you should never, under any circumstances, give any feedback to the candidate after the interview. If you do, you run the risk of not only getting a rebuttal from the candidate but also of revealing your selection strategy.

In the interview process, providing the candidate with your selection criteria or providing the candidate with a critique of how he or she measures up against it can prove disastrous. Don't do it!

Follow the ethics of interviewing

Do not under any circumstances ask the candidate to reveal any information that may be proprietary to past employers. In the interview process it happens all too frequently that candidates are brought in so that they can have their brains picked. Don't do it. It is improper, unethical, and could prove to be embarrassing to both you and your firm. Play it straight. Conduct your interviews for the sole purpose of filling jobs. Do not compromise your standards.

Always be courteous

Regardless of whether the candidate fares well or poorly during the selection process, treat him or her with respect and dignity. My motto has always been "Make a friend for my company, make a friend for myself." That motto has always enabled me to treat another person as I would want to be treated if I were in that person's shoes. It is an altogether proper way to run your operation.

Conduct worthwhile reference checks

If you are going to conduct reference checks, then you should endeavor to make them worthwhile. There are a number of do's and don'ts in this area. First of all, you will find that calling the references provided by the candidate is virtually worthless. No candidate in his or her right mind is going to furnish names that would provide anything but a glowing report.

Second, do not call the Personnel Department of the candidate's past employer. Personnel Departments usually have established policies and procedures for safeguarding information on previous employees, and as a result they will tell you very little. Many of them have a form that they will mail to you that requires you to obtain a written release from the former employee to obtain the information you seek. As a general rule, I usually avoid Personnel people when it comes to reference checks.

Who then, can you turn to? Very simple. The people

Employment Reference Check

Name of Applicant _____ For _____ Dept.

Position under consideration _____

Person contacted _____ Firm _____ Tele. _____

Employment period covered _____ From __/__ to __/__ Firm _____

----

1) In what capacity did you know the applicant and for how long? _____

2) What was his/her title? _____ What specifically did he/she do? _____

3) How would you rate his/her (a) performance? _____

    (b) Supervisory abilities? _____ Did his/her group like and respect him/her?

4) Creativity? _____ Worked independently? _____

5) How does he/she get along with others? _____ Work habits? _____

6) What were the circumstances surrounding his/her leaving? _____

Would you rehire him/her? Yes _____ Qualifications? _____

                             .No _____ Why? _____

7) What are his/her strengths or strong points? General _____

    Technical _____

8) Are there any negative aspects or weaknesses? _____

9) Probe suspected fault _____

10) Describe position under consideration and its requirements. Would you consider him/her suitable? _____

11) Any additional comments: _____

_____

_____

_____

                          Reference check made by _____

                          Date _____

who have the most information on the candidate and who are also far removed from the Personnel Department, namely past and/or present supervisors.

Here again, the value of having the applicant fill out an application form proves its value. The applicant will have to list past and present supervisors. These are the people to call.

The best way to perform the reference check is to ask the applicant for his or her permission to do so. Almost every applicant will willingly give you permission unless he or she has something to hide. Naturally, you would not call the applicant's current supervisor if the applicant has not informed the company that he or she is seeking other employment.

In making the reference checks, I have found it extremely useful to follow a checklist. A sample of a checklist that I have successfully used over the past several years is given on the preceding page. This can help you achieve a more structured and more thorough conversation. Any notes that you care to make can be made right on the checklist.

Equal employment opportunity and the legal implications of interviewing

With increasing frequency, employers are being subjected to costly law suits and settlements as a result of careless remarks made during interviews. All it takes to get into trouble with the law is to ask a single question that appears to be discriminatory. Please note that the question does not have to be discriminatory in and by itself. It only has to appear that way to the candidate. If you end up in court, the court will decide whether or not it was discriminatory. Don't let this happen to you. A good interview that allows you to make a good selection decision must also be a good interview in the sense that it reduces or eliminates the risk of any legal action arising out of it.

During the normal give and take of conversation, it is relatively easy to inadvertently ask a question or to make a remark that can be construed as discriminatory. To prevent this from happening you should be aware of the principles and laws that form the basis for today's equal employment opportunity program.

Affirmative action programs

With increasing frequency the federal government is requiring employers to "take affirmative action" to eliminate discrimination. In essence, this requires employers to make a specific effort to recruit persons in designated classifications, such as race, sex, and age, and to take positive action to ensure that such persons, when employed, have an equal opportunity for promotion and benefits.

Affirmative action programs cover certain groups of people in the United States that have suffered the effects of discrimination. The federal government has identified these groups and has designated them as "protected classes." The protected classes have been further defined as blacks, American Indians, handicapped persons (both physically and mentally), Spanish Americans (including Puerto Rican, Mexican-American, Cuban, Filipino, and all other Latin Americans), Spanish surnamed persons, women, and persons between the ages of 40 and 65.

Equal Employment Opportunity laws

There are many laws that deal with Equal Employment Opportunity. To present them all is beyond the scope of this book. I have, however, selected those laws that apply to virtually all employers. They represent the cornerstone of EEO legislation and will provide you with a solid background in this area.

Laws and executive orders

Although I don't intend to make you a legal wizard with regard to EEO laws, it is useful to be familiar with the federal and state laws and executive orders that call for equal opportunity and affirmative action. Hopefully, this will give you the necessary background to understand how these programs came into existence and why they play a significant role in today's reality.

THE EQUAL PAY ACT OF 1963 (ADDITION TO THE FAIR LABOR STANDARDS ACT OF 1938)

These two acts require employers to give men and women performing work in the same establishment under similar conditions the same pay, if their jobs require "equal skill . . . equal responsibility . . . equal effort." Jobs compared under the Equal Pay Act have to be substantially similar (for example, janitor and cleaning woman).

TITLE VII OF THE CIVIL RIGHTS ACT OF 1964, AS AMENDED BY TITLE VII OF THE CIVIL RIGHTS ACT OF 1972

The original Civil Rights Act of 1964 prohibited discrimination because of race, color, religion, sex, or national origin, in any term, condition, or privilege of employment. It also created the Equal Employment Opportunity Commission (EEOC) to enforce the act. The Civil Rights Act of 1972 strengthened the powers and expanded the jurisdiction of the EEOC in enforcement of this law.

THE AGE DISCRIMINATION IN EMPLOYMENT ACT OF 1967

This act prohibits all private employers of 25 or more persons from discriminating against persons aged 40 to 70 in any area of employment because of their age. It is designed to promote employment of older persons based on ability rather than age.

THE CIVIL RIGHTS ACT OF 1968

Title I of this act makes it a federal crime, punishable by fine and imprisonment, to intimidate, through the use of force or threat or threat of force, any persons on account of race, color, religion, or national origin, because he or she was enjoying, or was seeking to enjoy, the benefits of employment or the services of any union or employment agency.

Executive orders

These orders, issued by the president in 1965 and 1967, respectively, require affirmative action programs by all federal contractors and subcontractors, and require that firms with contracts over $50,000 and 50 or more employees develop and implement written programs, monitored by the Office of Federal Contract Compliance. These two orders require federal contractors to practice nondiscrimination in all aspects of their employment activity.

REVISED ORDER NO. 4

This order (issued in January, 1970, and later revised to include women in addition to minorities in its protected classes) spells out for federal contractors the specific requirements for their affirmative action programs. These requirements include identifying areas of minority and female "underutilization," listing numerical hiring and promotion goals, and taking other actions to remedy the effects of past discrimination or to counteract discriminatory barriers to equal employment.

EXECUTIVE ORDER 11141

This order states that it is the policy of the Federal government that government contractors and subcontractors shall not discriminate in employment on the basis of age. Congress has since legislated the ages from 40 to 70 as a protected class.

REHABILITATION ACT OF 1973

This act makes it illegal to discriminate against handicapped persons for jobs they are qualified to do.

This act and related laws call on all unions to represent employees fairly, impartially, and without discrimination. It also warns employers not to participate with unions, by action or inaction, in the commission of any discriminatory practices.

State and local laws

Many state and local laws prohibit employment discrimination. When the EEOC receives discrimination charges, it defers them for a limited time period (usually 180 days) to an EEOC-approved state agency with comparable jurisdiction and enforcement powers. If satisfactory remedies are not achieved, the EEOC takes back the case for resolution. Individuals and groups may also file dual discrimination complaints with federal and local agencies at the same time.

Other laws

Employment discrimination has also been ruled by courts to be prohibited by the Civil Rights Act of 1966 and 1970.

Agencies

In addition to state and local Fair Employment Practices Commissions that administer state laws, there are three main federal agencies/departments responsible for enforcing the laws and executive orders regarding affirmative action programs: the Department of Labor, the Equal Employment Opportunity Commission, and the Office of Federal Contract Compliance.

The Department of Labor

The Department of Labor, through its Wage and Hour Division, enforces the Equal Pay Act and the Age Discrimination Act.

The Equal Employment Opportunity Commission

The Equal Employment Opportunity Commission, established by Congress with the Civil Rights Act of 1964, enforces the provisions of that act. It has the authority to conduct investigations of employers and to file lawsuits in federal court if conciliation fails. Individual employees, themselves, or groups of employees, may also file charges with the EEOC and later bring lawsuits, if needed. Several employers have agreed to substantial back pay awards, wage adjustments, and other financial arrangements as a result of conciliatory agreement with the EEOC.

The Office of Federal Contract Compliance

The Office of Federal Contract Compliance (OFCC), established by the Department of Labor in the mid-1960s, enforces the regulations of executive orders 11246 and 11375. The OFCC is in charge of receiving and monitoring the EEO and affirmative action program reports submitted to it by federal contractors.

The government periodically conducts on-site compliance reviews of its contractors to ensure that affirmative action policies are being carried out. Failure to comply with the government orders and policies may mean termination or cancellation of federal contracts, inability to obtain future contracts, and/or the initiation of proceedings against the company by the EEOC or OFCC.

In the written affirmative action programs, the task of "analyzing" the work force, enumerating the job categories, and correcting any deficiencies found to exist is usually the responsibility of major facility management in conjunction with affirmative action personnel.

Standards

It may help to know some of the standards used to judge whether or not a practice is discriminatory. There are four prevalent standards used: the *chilling effect,* the *disparate impact theory,* the *perpetuating effect policies,* and the *statistical evidence theory.* There is also one "qualifier" to discrimination, the *bonafide occupational qualification,* which the courts sometimes allow employers to use in justifying a discriminatory practice.

The chilling effect

If a discriminatory employment practice has been eliminated from a company but the effects of that practice are continuing to prevent protected group applicants from applying for jobs, then positive steps must be taken to eliminate that "chilling effect" and to assure minorities and women that they are welcome in the company. Thus, simple elimination of a discriminatory practice does not automatically eliminate the effects of that practice.

The disparate impact theory

If an employment practice appears neutral on its face but is having a disproportionate effect on a certain protected segment or segments of the work force, then that policy is discriminatory. Similarly, employment policies that in theory apply equally to all employees are illegal if they discriminate against a certain protected segment or segments of the work force. For example, if you require a high school diploma of all job applicants, that policy is unfairly disqualifying a major portion of blacks and Spanish surnamed persons from applying for jobs, since those groups historically have not had equal educational opportunities. If, however, you can prove that a high school diploma or other job qualification is a necessity for successful job performance, the policy is still discriminatory, but it would not be illegal.

The perpetuating effect policies

Policies that perpetuate the effect of previous discriminatory practices are illegal. If a company at one time hired only white men but was ordered by the government to hire blacks and women, and then suffered a business slump forcing layoffs, blacks and women would be the first to go based on the company's seniority layoff policy.

The courts have ruled that straight seniority layoff systems and other systems that perpetuate the effects of previous discriminatory practices are unlawful and should be eliminated.

The statistical evidence theory

Statistics, such as a high number of one or more protected groups in a job category, constitute strong evidence of discriminatory practices. If you find such a situation exists in your organization, the responsibility will rest largely on you to show that the statistics are not the result of overt or institutional discrimination. For example, if you have ten women but only two men employed in your clerical area (even though there is a greater percentage of women than men in the labor force) you may be liable for a discrimination suit if you can't prove that there is a valid reason for all those women to be working in the same place. The burden of proof will rest largely on you.

Bonafide occupational qualification

Jobs, with extremely rare exceptions, are sexless. Also, there are no jobs that can be performed only by a single race or ethnic group. The bonafide occupational qualification (BFOQ) as to sex, which is claimed by many employers fighting discrimination suits, has been very narrowly interpreted by the EEOC and by the courts. There is no job that can be performed only by a single race. The EEOC has also concluded that labels such as "men's jobs" and "women's jobs" tend to deny employment opportunities unnecessarily to one sex or the other.

Pre-employment inquiries

The federal government and almost all states do not have published guides on pre-employment inquiries. Those government agencies, however, can request proof that any such inquiries are necessary to the screening of applicants and are not used for a discriminatory purpose. Two specific federal regulations cover age and sex:

- "Date of birth" or "age" can be requested but must be accompanied by a statement such as, "Both federal and state laws prohibit discrimination because of age."

- "Male," "Female," or "Mr., Mrs., or Miss" are not considered improper questions.

Two specific areas of inquiry are viewed with great suspicion by U. S. agencies:

- While not specifically prohibited, any questions about arrests will be challenged unless justified as a "business necessity."

- Questions about marital status and ages of children

171

will be challenged, particularly if only women are questioned.

In reviewing the affirmative action programs required of U. S. government contractors, antidiscrimination agencies have challenged many of the questions commonly included on applications such as "height, weight, previous address, and home ownership," as not job related.

The following are guidelines that seem to reflect the general thinking of all anti-discrimination agencies:

- cannot ask about change of name, nor maiden name of applicant's wife but can ask a married applicant for her maiden name

- cannot ask about birthplace before hire

 - can ask if applicant is a citizen and, if not, whether applicant is permitted to work in the U.S.A.; no questions permitted as to how citizenship was obtained

- cannot ask questions as to applicant's family

- can ask if U.S. veteran but not about military service for other countries; questions about nature of discharge have been challenged as similar in effect to arrest questions

- no limitation on education except as to inquiry about religious nature of educational institution

- no limitation on inquiring about previous experience

- religion is a forbidden topic

 - height and weight are permitted but complexion is prohibited; color of eyes and hair are frowned upon

- photographs cannot be requested or suggested on a voluntary basis before hiring

- permitted to ask about language and fluency but no inquiry as to how learned

- cannot ask for list of "all" organizations unless you indicate applicant may exclude those of a racial or religious character; can ask specifically about the Communist party (despite recent U.S. Supreme Court decision on Communist party, this is still a valid question)

- cannot ask for pastor or other religious references.

The best way to avoid any question of impropriety on application blanks or pre-hiring interviews is to eliminate all improper questions on the application blank and to provide for the collection of necessary information for insurance, physical check, security, and so forth, on a separate post-employment form.

Index

175